797,885 Books

are available to read at

www.ForgottenBooks.com

Forgotten Books' App
Available for mobile, tablet & eReader

ISBN 978-1-333-87536-7
PIBN 10695506

This book is a reproduction of an important historical work. Forgotten Books uses state-of-the-art technology to digitally reconstruct the work, preserving the original format whilst repairing imperfections present in the aged copy. In rare cases, an imperfection in the original, such as a blemish or missing page, may be replicated in our edition. We do, however, repair the vast majority of imperfections successfully; any imperfections that remain are intentionally left to preserve the state of such historical works.

Forgotten Books is a registered trademark of FB &c Ltd.
Copyright © 2017 FB &c Ltd.
FB &c Ltd, Dalton House, 60 Windsor Avenue, London, SW19 2RR.
Company number 08720141. Registered in England and Wales.

For support please visit www.forgottenbooks.com

1 MONTH OF FREE READING

at

www.ForgottenBooks.com

By purchasing this book you are eligible for one month membership to ForgottenBooks.com, giving you unlimited access to our entire collection of over 700,000 titles via our web site and mobile apps.

To claim your free month visit:

www.forgottenbooks.com/free695506

* Offer is valid for 45 days from date of purchase. Terms and conditions apply.

English
Français
Deutsche
Italiano
Español
Português

www.forgottenbooks.com

Mythology Photography **Fiction** Fishing Christianity **Art** Cooking Essays Buddhism Freemasonry Medicine **Biology** Music **Ancient Egypt** Evolution Carpentry Physics Dance Geology **Mathematics** Fitness Shakespeare **Folklore** Yoga Marketing **Confidence** Immortality Biographies Poetry **Psychology** Witchcraft Electronics Chemistry History **Law** Accounting **Philosophy** Anthropology Alchemy Drama Quantum Mechanics Atheism Sexual Health **Ancient History** **Entrepreneurship** Languages Sport Paleontology Needlework Islam **Metaphysics** Investment Archaeology Parenting Statistics Criminology **Motivational**

A Tour in the Highlands and Western Islands

"Dr John Leyden, a name which will not be soon forgotten in Scottish Literature."
—Sir Walter Scott.

"I never heard Scott name Leyden but with an expression of regard and a moistening eye."
—Allan Cunningham.

Journal of a Tour
in the
Highlands and Western Isla[n]ds of Scotland in 1800

BY

JOHN LEYDEN

EDITED, WITH A BIBLIOGRAPHY, BY

JAMES SINTON

WILLIAM BLACKWOOD AND SONS
EDINBURGH AND LONDON
1903

PREFATORY NOTE.

A CENTURY has now passed away since Dr John Leyden left Scotland for India, there to acquire, by the power of his wonderful genius, a foremost place in Oriental learning. He published, a few months before his departure for the East, in 1803, *Scotish Descriptive Poems*, and later in the same year, *Scenes of Infancy, Descriptive of Teviotdale*. In the preface to the former he says: "The Editor dismisses this little volume from his hands with mingled pleasure and regret: pleasure, from the recollection of several agreeable hours spent in its arrangement, during the intervals of severer study; and regret at bidding adieu to the investigation of Scotish literary antiquities, a subject which he can never expect to resume."

The present time, therefore, seems appropriate for the publication of his *Tour in the Highlands and Western Islands of Scotland in* 1800, the manuscript of which came into my hands about two years ago. It consists of 152 closely-written pages, commences in the form of a journal, and is continued in the character of letters addressed to his literary friends in Edinburgh,—Sir Walter (then Mr) Scott; Dr Robert Anderson, editor and biographer of the *British Poets;* Dr Thomas Brown, afterwards Professor of Moral Philosophy in the University of Edinburgh; and J. R., probably his early college friend James Reddie. The volume is neatly bound in russia, and has the appearance of having been preserved with great care. Beyond the fact that it was purchased at Messrs Sotheby's rooms, London, about four or five years ago, I have been able to discover nothing of its former owners, nor is there anything in the volume itself to throw any light on its history.

The tour was begun on July 14, and continued till October 1, 1800. In the Journal, now printed for the first time, Dr Leyden has collected a great deal of valuable information regarding the literary antiquities and traditions of the Highlands. Many curious observations also appear on the Ossian controversy, which still exercised the literati of the time.

Sir Walter Scott, Leyden's valued friend and biographer, has left on record an interesting account of this Journal. In his Memoir, originally published in *The Edinburgh Annual Register* for 1811, and afterwards reprinted in his *Miscellaneous Prose Works*, he says: "The autumn of the same year [1800] was employed in a tour to the Highlands and Hebrides, in which Leyden accompanied two young foreigners who had studied at Edinburgh the preceding winter. In this tour he visited all the remarkable places of that interesting part of his native country, and, diverging from the common and more commodious route, visited what are called the *rough bounds* of the Highlands, and investigated the decaying traditions of Celtic manners and story which are yet preserved in the wild districts of Moidart and Knoidart. The journal which he made on this occasion was a curious monument of his zeal and industry in these researches, and contained much valuable information on the subject of Highland manners and traditions, which is now probably lost to the public. It is remarkable that, after long and painful research in quest of original passages of the poems of Ossian, he adopted an opinion more favourable to their authenticity than has lately prevailed in the literary world. But the confessed infidelity of Macpherson must always excite the strongest suspicion on this subject. Leyden composed, with his usual facility, several detached poems upon Highland traditions, all of which have probably perished, excepting a ballad founded upon the romantic legend respecting Macphail of Colonsay and the Mermaid of Corrievrekin, inscribed to Lady Charlotte Campbell, and published in the third volume of the *Border Minstrelsy*, which appeared at the distance of about a twelvemonth after the two first volumes of that work.

The opening of this ballad exhibits a power of numbers which, for the mere melody of sound, has seldom been excelled in English poetry."

Sir Arthur Mitchell, in his delightful paper* read before the Society of Antiquaries, April 8, 1901, points out how important a place Tours form in the literature of a country, supplying, as they often do, information not to be found in ordinary histories. This remark is peculiarly applicable to the present work, as Leyden, no ordinary observer, has, with his usual ardour, recorded in these pages many incidents relating to the Highlands at a most interesting period.

It should perhaps be added that Dr Leyden's spelling of place-names in his

* *A List of Travels, Tours, Journeys, Voyages, Cruises, Excursions, Wanderings, Rambles, Visits, &c., relating to Scotland.* By Sir Arthur Mitchell, K.C.B., M.D., LL.D. *Proceedings of the Society of Antiquaries of Scotland*, vol. xxxv. pp. 431-638.

Journal has been followed throughout: most of them, however, will be easily identified by those familiar with the various districts visited. It has been my desire to present this Tour to the public as it was written by the author, often in circumstances of difficulty and discomfort.

The Bibliography appended to the Tour will, I trust, be found useful by those who are admirers of the life and writings of the illustrious scholar and poet. I have endeavoured to make it as complete as possible; but I shall feel grateful to any who may be in possession of books or MSS. by Dr Leyden not mentioned in my list, if they will kindly communicate with me on the subject.

To those friends who have interested themselves in this work I have to return my sincere thanks; and while not forgetful of their help, my special thanks are due to Dr Thomas Morton, London, but for whose kind assistance the manuscript portion of the Bibliography would have been very incomplete. To Dr John Morton, Guildford, I am also under a deep debt of gratitude for furnishing me with a list of Leyden MSS. in his possession; and I must not omit to record my indebtedness to Mr A. H. Millar, Dundee; Mr Charles H. Tawney, M.A., C.I.E., India Office, Whitehall; Dr John Leyden Morton, London; and Mr William Macmath, Edinburgh, for assistance received in the Bibliographical portion of this work.

J. S.

January 1903.

CONTENTS.

JOURNAL.

PAGE

July 14. Edinburgh to Kirkliston—Niddry Castle—Linlithgow—Falkirk—Carron Park—Museum at Kinnaird House—Bruce's Abyssinian MSS.—Bannockburn—Stirling . . . 1

July 15. Stirling Castle—Rev. James Somerville, D.D.—Mr Ramsay of Ochtertyre—Blair-Drummond—Doune Castle—River Keltie—Callander—River Teith 7

July 16. Loch Venachoir—The Water-Horse—Loch Achray—Trosachs—Loch Katrine—Mrs Murray of Kensington—Den of the Ghost—Coilichrah—Loch Arkulet—Fort of Inversnaid 12

July 17. Tarbet—Ben Lomond—Loch Lomond . 17

July 18. Loch Long—Arthur Seat—Glen Croe—Rest-and-be-Thankful—Glen Kinglass—Arkinglass—Loch Fyne—Inveraray—Captain Archibald Campbell 21

July 19. Inveraray Castle—Duke of Argyle—Hill of Duniquiech—Glen Aray—Glen Shirah—Dr Robertson—Dhu-loch—Sir John MacGregor Murray—Sir William Hart's MS. *Journal of a Tour through the Crimea* . 25

July 20. Loch Awe—Bunawe—Loch Etive 28

CONTENTS

July 21. Oban — Dunolly Castle — Dunstaffnage Castle—Boiling well—M. Berlepoch—Auchnacraig 31
July 22. Druidic circle—Dowart Castle—Church of Strachale—Aros—Loch-na-gaul . . . 34
July 23. German friends visit Staffa . . . 36
July 24. Ulva—Staffa—Long Cave—Boo-shalla —Cave of Fingal—Iona — The Abbey — St Oran's Chapel—The Nunnery—Hi—Dun-i— Sound of Fechan—Mull—Carsaig Bay—Story of MacPhail of Colonsay—The Mermaid of Corrivrekin 37
July 25. Oban—Baron Vincke—Mr Burgsdorff— Sir Francis D'Ivernois 50
July 26. Easdale—Slate quarries—Loch Fechan —Clachan 54
July 27. Loch Crinan—Resave—Sound of Jura— Whirlpool of Corrivrekin—Duntroon Castle Loch Gilpin—Oakfield House . . . 55
July 28. Loch Gilpin-head — Mr Campbell of Ashkenish—Loch Gair House—Loch Glaissean—Provost Campbell of Inveraray—Miss Betty Campbell 61
July 29. Commissary Campbell of Ross — Loch Salenughellaghelly—Taynish—Loch Swein . 64
August 6. Mrs Campbell—Miss Lamont—Anecdotes respecting Duntroon's March — Dun Vourich—Castle Sueno—Elen-mor-macoharmaig—Legendary stories concerning ancient crosses—Macoharmaig's study—Isla—Scarba —Paps of Jura—Rui Bhrettanich—Prospect Hill—Mr Gow—Mr Malcolm—Kilmartine— Carnassary Castle—Bishop Carswell—Proverb expressive of his avarice 66
August 7. Duntroon Castle—Loch Crinan-side— Manufacture of kelp—Distillation of whiskey 77

LETTERS.

August 11. *To Dr Robert Anderson.* Bunawe—Dalmally—Muckairn—Pass of Brander—Glenorchy—River Awe—Barra Castle—Barran—Mr MacNab—Poems of Ossian—Loch Awe—Kilchurn Castle—Legend respecting Sir Colin Campbell—Castle Fraoch Elan—Inishail—History of the MacGregor proscription—Ben Cruachan—Gaelic proverb 80

August 15. *To Dr Thomas Brown.* Site of ancient Berigonium—Lismore—Rev. Mr MacNicol—"Lochaber no more"—Gaelic traditions—Round tower—Fingal's territories—Observations on poems attributed to Ossian—MacVurich's MSS.—Poems of Ossian before they were translated by MacPherson — *Ur-sgeuls* or New Tales—Highland legends—Gaelic song 100

August 16. *To J. R.* Island of Kerrera—Tradition relating to brooch of Lorn—Horse Shoe Harbour—Gylen Castle 116

August 20. *To Dr Robert Anderson.* Appin—Ancient territory of the Stuarts—Proverbs regarding the Clans Campbell, MacDougal, and Cumming—Connal Ferry—Shian Ferry—Port Appin—Portnacroish—Linnhe Lisach—Airds House—Castle of Appin—Castle Stalker—Rev. Mr MacColl—Tradition regarding tombstone of a Danish prince—Ballahulish—Beniveir—Captain Stuart—Glenco—Ruins of ancient mansion where MacDonald was murdered—Lochaber—Lochleven—River Co—Massacre of Glenco—Poems of Ossian . 121

August 23. *To Walter Scott.* Catholics of Moideart—Inversanda—Glen Tarbet—Loch Sunairt—Morven—Ardnamurchan—Strontian—Mr Patience—London House—Mr Wilson—Loch Shiel—Pollock—Mr Hope—Ben Rusepol—

Moss of Kintra—Dalilie—Captain A. MacDonald — Samlaman — Elan Shona — Mr A. MacDonald—Loch Moideart—Kinloch Moideart—Tyrim Castle—MacDonald of the Isles 138

August 27. *To Walter Scott.* Penibhely—Isle of Canna—Sky—Arisaig—Loch Ailort—Prince Charles—Isle of Egg—Cave of massacre—Traditionary account of the massacre—Scouregg—Isle of Muck—Rum—Morar—Knoydart—Rev. Mr MacLean—Slate—Mr Martin MacPherson—Mr MacDonald of Tormor—Armidale—Elan Dermid—Glenelg . 152

August 30. *To J. R.* Loch Nevis—Islandrioch—Round towers of Carron—Rev. Mr Downie—Ossian's Poems—Battle of the Fingalians—Mr MacLeod of Islandrioch—Gaelic Dictionary—Mr MacDonell of Scothouse—Mr Gillespie—Ancient wicker houses—MacDonell of Glengarry—Mainclach-aird—Glen Dessery—Loch Arkeig—Auchnacarrie—Loch-Eil—Fassefern—Inverlochy Castle—Gordonsburgh—Fort William 167

September 3. *To Dr Robert Anderson.* Ben Nevis—Mr Cameron of Glen Nevis—Captain Cameron—Mr Grant of Glen Urquhart—Highbridge—River Spean—MacDonells of Keppoch—Glen Roy—Parallel Roads—Traditionary report of their use—Pass of Corryarrick—Badenoch—Loch Gary—Fort Augustus—Abertarff—Strath Errick—Glen Morrison—Loch Ness—Fall of Fyres—House of Fyres—General's Hut—Urquhart Castle—Mealfourvounie—Black Rock—Dochfour—Tom-na-heurich 183

September 11. *To Dr Robert Anderson.* Inverness—Muirtown—Craig Phadrick—Vitrified forts—Forts of Duncan, Macbeth, and Oliver Cromwell—Beauley River—Red Castle—Provost Inglis—Ossian's Poems—Highland antiquities—Rellich—Glen Beg—Culloden House—

CONTENTS

Culloden Moor — Druidic circle — Captains Clunes and Brown—Castle Stewart—Campbelton—Fort George—Moray Firth—Moor where Macbeth met the witches . . . 207

September 19. *To Dr Robert Anderson.* Nairn—Inchoch—Brodie—Dalvey—Darnaway Castle —Findhorn—Forres—Ancient obelisk—Kinlossie Abbey—Elgin—The Abbey—Fochabers —River Spey—Strathspey—Castle Gordon —Balrinnes—Keith—New Mills—Braes of Balloch—River Deveron—Huntly—Leith Hall —Major-General Hay—Strathbogie—Garioch —Hill of Noth—Vitrified fort—Hill of Benachie — Kildrummie — Drumennir Tower — Rhynie—Den of Craig—Miss A. Gordon—Castle of Craig—Ballad of *Edom o' Gordon* —Buck of the Cabroch—Kildrummie Castle —Strath of Don—Dunedeir—Vitrified fort —Christ's Kirk—Inverury—Battle of Harlaw —Aberdeen—The quay—Dialect . . . 218

September 24. *To Dr Robert Anderson.* Aberdeen —Ancient cross—King's College—Marischal College — Professors Gerard, Jack, Brown, Glennie, and Kidd—College libraries—Bibliographic enquiries—Curious MSS.—*Albania* —River Dee—Kincardine O'Neil—Pass of Ballater—Braemar—Mineral springs of Pannanich—Dee Castle—Braemar Castle—Castletown—Gaelic of Braemar—Mar Lodge—Glen Beg—Glenshee—Mar Forest—Strathmore—Marly—Loch Drumelzie—Loch Stormont—Black Loch—White Loch—Loch Finess—Loch Ree—Loch Dramalie—Loch Clunie—Loch Butterston—Loch of the Lows—Admirable Crichton—Dunkeld—The Cathedral—White Crag—Atholl House—Ossian's Hall—River Braan—Rumbling Linn 238

September 30. *To Dr Robert Anderson.* River Tay — Logierait — River Tummel — Dalguise —Kinnaird—Fascalie—Fall of the Tummel

—Pass of Killiecrankie—Blair Atholl—Lude—Atholl Castle—River Tilt—Falls of the Bruar—Duke of Atholl—Rev. Mr MacLaggan—Highland antiquities—Gaelic poems in MS.—Poems of Ossian—Loch Tummel—Loch Tummel Castle—Sheehallion—Strath-Tay—Castle Garth—Loch Tay—Kenmore—Killin—Ben Lawers—Kinnell—Druidic circle—Rivers Lochy and Dochart—Fall of the Dovecraig—Fall of Acharn—Taymouth—Druidic circle—Aberfeldie—Weem—Moness—Fascalie—Bishoprick—Murthly—Delvin—Stenton—Birnam—Stanley—Taymount—Linn of Campsie—Kinclaven Castle—Scone—The Palace—St Martins—Dunsinan Hill—Gowrie Castle—Mr Morison 252

October 1. *To Dr Thomas Brown.* Perth—Kinnoul Crags—Kinfauns—Carse of Gowrie—Firth of Tay—Strathearn—River Earn—Abernethy—Brig of Earn—Ochil Hills—Loch Leven—The Castle—Kinross House—Kinross . 272

NOTES 279
BIBLIOGRAPHY 285

TOUR IN THE HIGHLANDS.

July 14, 1800.—From Edinburgh to Linlithgow we traversed a flat uninteresting district, where the hills which confined our view presented nothing picturesque, and the groups which the valleys exhibited were extremely insipid. A distant prospect of the Ochil hills on our right, and occasional glimpses of the Forth, were all that diversified the scene; so to relieve its uniformity we talked of the wild districts of Germany and Bohemia, and enjoyed a comfortable degree of that wise passiveness which is undisturbed by reflection, and suffers the uninteresting images of things to glide over the mind as over a mirror. The ruin of Niddry Castle, situated beyond Kirkliston at the termination of a clump of trees, is the only picturesque object.

From Linlithgow to Falkirk the view is equally uniform and equally confined. The copses of trees are more numerous, and the ridges and declivities of the Ochil hills appear more distinctly. Falkirk seems to be much inferior to Linlithgow in regularity, though it contains perhaps some better edifices, but the want of a castle incapacitates it completely from contending with Linlithgow in respectability. From Falkirk we passed on to Carron Park, and had a view of the works of Carron *en passant.* I only mean the exterior buildings, however, for though we heard the sound of hammers and saw the smoke ascending of a fiery red colour, we saw nothing more belonging to the

Cyclops' den. At Carron Park we had a beautiful view of the large reservoir for Carron works. The canal—which extends about thirty-five miles in length, at a medium breadth of about twenty-four feet and depth of ten—presents a very agreeable diversity by exhibiting vessels sailing through fine copses of wood, with the masts glimmering through the trees. By favour of Mr Cadell of Carron Park, we had a view of the very curious museum formed at Kinnaird by Abyssinian Bruce. I was pleased to find the most unequivocal proofs of his journey to Abyssinia, and of his acquaintance with Abyssinian manners and literature. Besides numerous drawings of animals, birds, fishes, and plants which have never been engraved, we saw twenty-four vols. MSS. in Ethiopic, with some very elegant specimens of Ethiopic writing by Mr Bruce.

The Abyssinian MSS. consist of: *History of Abyssinia*, 6 vols.; *Chronicle of Axum*, 2 vols.; *Abyssinian Constitutions*, 1 vol.; *Old and New Testament*, 9 vols.; *Apostolical History*, 2 vols.; *The Synaxar, or Lives of the Saints*, 4 vols.

This circumstance ought entirely to silence the idle cavils and objections which have been urged against the authenticity of the second volume of his travels extracted from the Abyssinian annals.*

Among Mr Bruce's specimens of Ethiopic I saw part of a vocabulary which he had formed of the Amharic; also Leon's *Historicale Description de*

* Subsequent to this period, and before Dr Leyden left for India in 1803, he had been consulted on the subject of the posthumous edition of Mr Bruce's travels, which his friend Dr Alexander Murray afterwards edited. See Murray's *History of the European Languages*, &c., with Life of the Author. Vol. i. Edin., 1823. Pp. lxxix-lxxxii, note.

l'Afrique, 1556; *Histoire Geographique de l'Egypte* (*Arab*), 3 vols. 4to; the Coptic MS. on papyrus, still very legible, which Mr Bruce asserts to be a Gnostic production—boards almost like a modern book; also the Tot found at Axum, inscribed with hieroglyphics apparently in their last stage; and a cast in stucco inscribed with hieroglyphics.

It is impossible to particularise all the antiques, though many of them are very curious.

I viewed with some degree of respect the quadrant and timepiece which had accompanied him to Abyssinia, and the cup with which he drank his Majesty's health at the source of the Nile.

There are some exquisite specimens of petrifaction, particularly a very fine agate, the fracture of which resembles the joint of the foreleg of an ox both in colour and in delicate polish.

There are likewise some very beautiful specimens of that kind of transmuted rather than petrified wood which preserves the form of a tree and exhibits the reticulations of the bark, with tints of charcoal. The species of wood might have been determined from these reticulations.

From Kinnaird we proceeded by Torwoodhead to Stirling. I approached Bannockburn with such vivid emotions of patriotism, that had an Englishman presented himself I should have felt strongly inclined to knock him down. The subsiding of this martial enthusiasm left me in a high poetical key, which probably increased the effect which the view of Stirling and the castle, with the declivity wooded to the very wall and in some places apparently surmounting the ramparts, might have naturally produced. When we reached Stirling we immediately ascended the castle, after waiting on the Rev. Mr Somerville,* whom we did not find at home. The view to the west is extremely beautiful, though not equal to that down the Forth, the meanders of which were hardly discernible through the haze of the evening. On returning to the inn we found a card from Mr Somerville inviting us to breakfast, which we accepted.

July 15.—We rose early in the morning and ascended the castle hill, from which we surveyed the beautiful vale of the Forth, the meanders of which river almost exceed imagination. They are finely described by MacNeill in his *Links of Forth*. I was particularly

---

* Rev. James Somerville, D.D., minister first of the Scottish Church at Rotterdam (1775-1779), then at Whitburn (1779-1789). He was inducted to the second charge of the parish of Stirling, October 8, 1789, and to the first, June 27, 1793. He died January 23, 1817.

pleased with one rock, to which the windings of the river almost extended. It had a striking resemblance to Salisbury Crags, but the declivity at the foot of the precipice was covered with wood instead of loose stones. We walked round the castle, and examined the rock on which it is founded. It is basaltic, but, probably from an over proportion of iron, many of the columns are in a state of decomposition.

We breakfasted with Mr Somerville's family. That gentleman, whose character I much admire, is a stern Calvinist in opinion, and extremely ready to enter upon the defence of the good old cause. The town of Stirling contains many good edifices, but is very inelegant and irregular.

From Stirling we proceeded to Ochtertyre, the seat of Mr Ramsay,* a gentle-

* The friend of Sir Walter Scott and patron of Robert Burns. A selection from his manuscripts

man well versed in the history of Scotish literature, as is demonstrated by his strictures on Scotish literature in Dr Currie's edition of Burns's Works. After visiting his Salictum,* an elegant Latin inscription for which is published in that work,

> Nine times o'er we viewed the garden,
> And saw it was not worth a farthing.

The walk by the side of the river Forth is indeed extremely beautiful, and deeply shaded with trees. We had a good deal of conversation concerning Scotish songs and literature, Ossian's poems, &c.

Mr Ramsay mentioned that Dr Stewart of Luss had never been able

---

was published in 1888, entitled *Scotland and Scotsmen in the Eighteenth Century. From the MSS. of John Ramsay, Esq. of Ochtertyre.* 2 vols. Edited by Alexander Allardyce.

* "A willow walk on the banks of the Teith, within the grounds of Ochtertyre."

to hear a dozen of lines of Ossian in the wildest parts of the Highlands, where foreigners had hardly penetrated. He stated that customs were alluded to in Ossian which he believed were unknown to Mr MacPherson, but of the latter part of the argument no satisfactory proof was mentioned. *Vide* Ramsay's Dissertation on Funeral Rites and on Scotish Poetry and Music before Macdonald's 'Airs.'

After leaving Ochtertyre we passed Blair-Drummond, and viewed the water-wheel which raises the water of the river, which is conducted to the moss of Kincardine to be employed for the clearing of that unproductive ground by a very singular species of agriculture. We had an imperfect view of these operations, yet such as conveyed a very correct idea of them.

At the water-wheel we met two Germans—Baron Vincke, a little gruff personage, who smoked his pipe with great composure, Burgsdorff, and D'Ivernois, a Genevois. They seemed all very intent upon acquiring an accurate acquaintance with the agriculture of the country. They only accompanied us to the Teith, a beautiful river well wooded. We had a view of the Castle of Doune, an ancient pile in ruins, which we approached to examine. It seems to have consisted of two large towers joined on both sides by a strong wall connected with the exterior edifices. As we approached Callander the scenery became more wild: the green tints of the hills disappeared, and the brown heath supplied their place. Before us Ben Lomond, Ben Cruchan [Cruachan], and Ben Ledi towered to the clouds, while the sunbeams descended in confined straight lines on the head of the last.

We passed the Keltie, a small but

beautiful river, and arrived at Callander, a neat regular village, which has a striking resemblance to Copshawholm, on the banks of the Liddell. It is larger, however, and some of the houses are not so new. The range of rocks on the north is extremely beautiful. At a distance it seems basaltic, and is fringed with trees, which rise in successive gradations.

We walked along the Teith in the evening to examine the vestiges of a Roman camp. I must confess, however, that they were by no means striking, and we saw nothing which determined them to be Roman.

July 16.—We left Callander about nine in the morning, with Ben Ledi full in front, shaggy with dun heath and gray rocks, and winding to the left round its foot, soon came in sight of Loch Venachoir, *the fair valley.* It is bounded by high mountains which slope considerably from the border of the lake, slightly fringed with wood along their base. It struck me as resembling Leathes water considerably, only the character of the scenery is darker, from the heath of the surrounding hills. As we saw no ripe corn, we could not judge of its effect; but in its naked state it does not deserve its name. Our guide informed us that the people of the vale had been a good deal alarmed by the appearance of that unaccountable being the water-horse (*Each Uisge**) during the spring, which had not been seen there since the catastrophe of Corlevrann, *the wood of woe*, when he carried into the loch fifteen children who had broken Pace Sunday. I made enquiries concerning the habits of the animal, and was only able to learn that its colour

* See Note A, p. 279.

was brown, that it could speak, and that its motion agitated the lake with prodigious waves, and that it only emerged in the hottest midday to be on the bank.

We next reached Loch-a-chravy [Loch Achray] and passed the rivulet which issues from Glenfinglas, a dark solemn glen shut up by a forest, chiefly of oak, with rocks towering above the tops of the trees. The rocks, or rather hills, around Loch-a-chravy are jagged, broken, and irregular, and the lake itself is only seen by glimpses through the wood which confines the road. At the upper end of the lake the Trosachs present themselves, a cluster of wonderful rocks which shut up the defile of Loch Ketterin.* They display a most astonishing and savage mixture of gray precipices huddled together in awful confusion, projecting with bare and

* See Note B, p. 280.

woody points, intermingling with and surmounting each other, wedging into each other's sides, and patched in the most fantastic manner by brown heath finely contrasted with the verdure of the trees. The precipices are dreadfully rent and torn. The gloom and the silence of the place cause every footfall to be echoed far and wide. As we wound silently through this confusion of beauty and horror, we soon heard the sounds of the waves dying away among the rocks. The south end of the lake is finely diversified by islands and woody promontories, but in some places, from the quantity of wood that has been cut down, the sides of the rock have been left bare and naked, by which the solemn effect is much diminished, as we were informed by Mrs Murray of Kensington,* whom we were fortunate enough to meet just

* See Note C, p. 281.

as we came in sight of the lake. She conducted us to Murray Point, named from herself, the discoverer; whence we had an enchanting view of part of the Trosachs and of the greater part of the lake, the precipice of the Den of the Ghost, and the Peak of Rutting or Stuic-a-chroin. The sides of the lake are beautifully fringed with wood, above which a dun expanse of unbroken heath ascends almost to the top of the hills, where it is surmounted by broken ranges of rocks. We proceeded along the lake to Auch-mach-munh, where we intended to take a boat and ferry over, but the lake was too rough. We therefore proceeded to Coilichrah, where we procured a boat from Mr Macfarlane and sent round our horses by Glengyle. The rocks on the side of Loch Ketterin are chiefly alpine schistus indurated, often containing a considerable quantity of micaceous particles. There are some precipices of granite among the Trosachs.

The road between Loch Ketterin and Loch Lomond winds by the side of a small lake called Loch Arkulet, the sides of which are naked and bleak. Ben Lomond appeared crested with mist; there was little diversity of scenery. We passed the strong house of Ben Snedh [Fort of Inversnaid], where a small garrison was formerly kept, and reached the north side of Loch Lomond, which we crossed, and after a delightful sail arrived at Tarbet.

July 17.—Tarbet is a small straggling village, containing, however, a good inn kept by Mr Macfarlane. Having taken a boat, we sailed along the shore of the lake for a considerable time, as the top of the mountain Ben Lomond was enveloped in mist. As there was no prospect of its dispersing, we landed on a round promontory opposite Tarbet and began to ascend the hill.

From the first great ledge of the mountain the opposite shore appears bordered with white sand and fringed with wood, chiefly oak, and consequently displaying little diversity of tint. Glen Tarbet [leads] away towards Loch Long, and winds off towards Glen Croe. The hills above Tarbet are of a uniform brown aspect, with few trees, and only jagged with rocks at the summit.

When we arrived at the second ledge the mist still crested the top of the mountain, the head of Loch Long still presented itself, and Loch Sloy appeared in a rocky valley elevated far above Loch Lomond. The view of the latter lake towards the south is surprisingly beautiful.

The eastern shore displays a waving undulated outline, while the western is steep and little indented. The lake shone like silver in the beams of the sun, and was beautifully diversified with numerous islands, green and covered with wood. From the north side a romantic promontory stretched far into the water. Beyond the lake we saw the water of Clyde, and between them the Castle of Dumbarton towers upon a lofty rock. Ranges of hills begin to tower beyond those which overhang.

We advanced to the top of the mountain through a very close mist, and meeting some gentlemen descending, we were told that we might possibly see as far as our arms' length. Undeterred, we ascended the summit; and while we were examining the rocks in a very disconsolate manner, suddenly a vast chasm opened in the surrounding fog and we saw distinctly Glen Tarbet and part of Loch Lomond, and as the mist rolled away in broken columns and irregular fleeces, we had a fine prospect of the southern part of the lake and its island, and soon after we saw the Forth and some small lakes on the tops of the low heathy hills, with a considerable part of Loch Ketterin. The columns of white mist then descended rapidly in all directions through the defiles of the mountains, and closing in an immense ocean, like the waves of the Red Sea round the Israelites, left for a time the tops of the hills swimming like islands in the obscure white, and these were soon enveloped in total obscurity. This scene, which is extremely sublime, was several times repeated during our stay.

The only species of stones we observed were blue and white alpine schistus, extremely micaceous and sometimes ferruginous, and quartz, blue and white. In the middle of the mountain the schistus is most unmixed. We observed curious specimens of saxifrage.

Descending rapidly from the mountain we sailed considerably to the south of Tarbet, and had a view of the surrounding scenery from the lake, which increases the effect of the wood but diminishes greatly the effect of the rocks. The sides of the hills are neither so precipitous nor so steep as at the finest lakes of Cumberland.

July 18.—We left Tarbet this morning and proceeded to Loch Long, where the herring-fishery had commenced. This lake displays a fine sweep of water, bearing no inconsiderable resemblance to the northern part of Loch Lomond, and soon winds round a promontory shagged with wood. The hills on the right are of an uniform dun heath; their tops are irregular and rocky. The hill termed Arthur Seat has all the appearance of a ruptured volcano.

We left Loch Long and entered the vale of Glen Croe, the most desolate place under heaven. It is completely covered with stones of different descriptions, which leave no room for vegetation. It is generally involved in mist; but as we passed the day was clear enough to display all the horrors of the glen, which were, however, much relieved by the view of a merry sheep-shearing in the valley. The vale of Glen Croe is about five miles long, extremely narrow, and confined by steep declivities covered with loose stones and crested with immense broken precipices, which shut up every avenue to this valley of desolation except the entrance from Loch Long and the winding pass of Rest-and-be-Thankful, so called from an inscription which accurately delineates the feelings of the soldiers employed in constructing the military path through this sequestered region. During our passage my attention was attracted by the appearance of a cave, to which I clambered among some steep rocks, but found only a very shallow cavity.

Passing along the head of Glen Croe we entered the vale of Glen Kinglass, which does not present such numerous vestiges of desolation, though the hills are more lofty and towering. Their sides are covered with verdure to the bottom, but the tops consist of immense rugged precipices which rise in awful majesty over each other, and often present the appearance of the ruptured crater of a volcano. In gloomy majesty Glen Croe may be compared to Borrowdale, but Glen Kinglass is certainly vastly superior to Patterdale.

We emerged from Glen Kinglass at Arkinglass, the beautiful house of which stands upon Loch Fyne, and is well sheltered with wood. I ferried over the head of the lake, and had an admirable view of it from the head to the bay of Inveraray. The green hill which shelved away from Glen Kinglass is finely contrasted by a white rocky mountain opposite, the base of which is covered with wood, as is the dark heathy mountain on the opposite side of the lake over Glen Kinglass.

The approach to Inveraray is extremely beautiful at the opening of the bay, and at a distance the Gothic aspect of Inveraray Castle assimilates very well with the scene, though its round turrets and elevated dome bid defiance even to the rules of Gothic architecture. The village of Inveraray is built with considerable regularity, and the hills which rise beyond it are finely wooded. The vale of Glen Shirah, shaded with wood on the side of Duniquiech, and bounded on the other by a steep declivity, green at the base, and at the top covered with dark heath, is extremely beautiful. After arriving at Inveraray I waited on Captain Archibald Campbell, who conducted us through various beautiful walks in the Duke's policy, and carried us up a deep sequestered glen, termed the "mossy glen" in Gaelic, the steep declivities on the sides of which are entirely formed of loose rolling stones, chiefly of granite.

July 19.—We spent this day in surveying the environs of Inveraray, Inveraray Castle, and dining with the Duke of Argyle. The hill of Duniquiech has a most picturesque effect, being covered with wood to the top and surmounted by a small turret. The view is not so extensive as might be expected, but has considerable variety,—Loch Fyne and the hills beyond it, the town of Inveraray, Glen Shirah, and Glen Aray. The view from the leads of the castle is softer but not so extensive, as it neither includes Glen Shirah nor Glen Aray.

We walked about three miles up Glen Shirah with Dr Robertson, passed Dhu-loch, and examined the construction of the Duke's barn in that valley. It is constructed in the form of a semicircle, with numerous ventilators. The low story forms a double range of stalls for black cattle in winter. The floors of the upper stories are formed of boards placed at six inches' distance, and the walls and roofs are provided with wooden hooks for suspending sheaves of corn or bundles of hay, which are deposited green or new cut, and are soon dried in the wettest seasons. Glen Aray is better wooded than Glen Shirah, but has not such an extensive prospect.

We dined at the Duke's in company with Sir John MacGregor Murray, who was going on a tour to the Islands, partly to collect the evidence for the authenticity of Ossian's Poems, and to take the depositions of persons able to recite them or who had heard them recited.

Sir William Hart lent me for the evening a vocabulary of French, German, Polish, and Latin, printed at Warsaw in 1770, and his MS. *Journal of a Tour through the Crimea*, written in French. This tour, which it was almost impossible to render uninteresting, as it was performed in the months of June and July 1796, infinitely excels *Bubb Dodington's Diary*, and informs us with great accuracy when he rose in the morning, whether he reposed well, whether he got a good dinner, what wine he drank, and when he was forced to take *café noire faute de crême;* but as for the manners of the people, the antiquities, the aspect, the soil, and economy of the country, you may as well expect a decision of the question whether angels have beards. Sir William, however, promised to show me some medals with Greek inscriptions, which he picked up with his own hands among the ruins of a great city, when he returned to Edinburgh. The rocks round Inveraray are chiefly schistu granitæ and of limestone. We were told of a species of the latter which contains magnesia. The Lapis Ollaris abounds.

July 20.—We left Inveraray this morning, and proceeding up Glen Aray for some time, wound along the foot of a rocky mountain and passed a very wild heath with Bunawe full in our front till we reached Loch Awe. Bunawe towers above the adjoining ridges; the front is naked and covered with white rocks, while the base is shaggy with wood.

Loch Awe is extremely beautiful: the ample sweep of water, the bordering of deep green oak, the contrast of the white rocks of Bunawe and the dun heath and green declivities which enclose it on every side, the termination of the view at the head by an old castle apparently ruinous, and the division of the lake where one arm advances towards Loch Etive, render it superior to all but Loch Lomond and Loch Ketterin.

After crossing Loch Awe we soon reached a long glen, the sides of which are thickly covered, or rather concealed, by a forest of birch. I never saw that tree look so beautiful. There was rather too little variety in the tints of the wood, which climbed almost to the top of the neighbouring hills. The sides of the glen are irregular and picturesque, though they do not present any of the wild beauties of the Trosachs, and are entirely devoid of rocks. At * I examined an ancient tombstone of the Sinclairs. Some of the sculpture was in a good taste, as the flowers . . .†

I then proceeded along the side of Loch Etive, which is diversified with little variety of scenery, till I reached the cataract, as it is called, which fortunately happened to be in considerable perfection as I passed it. The ebbing of the tide in this lake, as it runs over a rocky shelf in its return to the sea, presents all the appearance

* Name omitted in MS.
† This sentence appears to have been added later and left incomplete.

of a rapid river descending down a steep declivity.

On the opposite side of Loch Etive I saw the supposed site of the ancient Berigonium, marked by rocks which have no resemblance to ruins. The ruins as well as the history of this city have perished, and it hardly lives in tradition. From the same spot I had a view of the ruins of Dunstaffnage Castle; but the evening closed rapidly round us and I hurried on to Oban.

July 21.—Oban is a small straggling village about the size of Inveraray, though much more irregular in the arrangement of the edifices of which it consists. The rocks in the neighbourhood are almost entirely plum-pudding stone and granite.

We walked up to Dunolly Castle, the ancient seat of the MacDougals, and examined the rocks along the shore.

Among the masses of plum-pudding stone I distinctly perceived some porous scoriæ of lava. The view of Dunolly Castle, or rather ruins, is eminently picturesque from the base of the precipice by the shore on the way to Oban, especially if a large mass of plum-pudding stone which stands erect be taken into the foreground.

From the top of the ruins we had a fine view of the adjacent isle of Kerrera, of Lismore, a dun level country, and of the more distant mountains of Mull and Morven.

From Dunolly we proceeded to Dunstaffnage, and viewed that immense pile of ruins. The castle, the walls of which are enormously thick and still in a high degree of preservation, consists of a large square like that of Bewcastle, but is a little more rounded at the corners. The echo—which is produced by a person speaking from the castle, who hears nothing himself and is heard by a person stationed at the chapel—is very singular.

On our way to Dunstaffnage we visited the remarkable boiling well, where the appearance of violent boiling is produced by the emission of air, but we did not see it in perfection.

At Oban we found M. Berlepoch, a Saxon lady, who seemed to be very amiable and very learned, and who, I understand, is both a poetical and political writer, but she was just on the eve of departure at our arrival.

On our return from Dunstaffnage we found our German friends Vincke and Burgsdorff arrived and ready to set out for Mull, and we immediately determined to accompany them. On account of the *maladie du mer*, Sir Francis D'Ivernois was forced to stay at Oban. The night was raw and misty, so that we could hardly distinguish the shore of Morven, and it was dark when we arrived at Auchnacraig.

July 22.—We left Auchnacraig this morning to traverse Mull, and at a mile's distance we saw what is termed a Druidic circle. The rocks which we saw during our journey along the shore were almost invariably composed of basalt. We saw one white porous stone of considerable levity, friable like burnt limestone. At Auchnacraig the threshold and some part of the house was floored with blue limestone dotted like pyrites, as if it had been stuck full of nails. We saw the ruins of Castle Dowart soon after leaving Auchnacraig. The huts of the peasants in Mull are most deplorable. Some of the doors are hardly four feet high, and the houses themselves, composed of earthen sods in many instances, are scarcely twelve. There is often no other outlet of smoke but at the door, the consequence of which is that the women are more squalid and dirty than the men, and their features more disagreeable. The hills are of considerable height and shagged with wood, but the land is extremely fertile. The food of the lower classes consists chiefly of potatoes, in the culture of which they are very expert. The young people generally devote themselves to a seafaring life. In the ruinous church of Strachale we saw a very ancient inscription almost obliterated. The Moresque flourish was in a very elegant taste.

At Aros we procured a guide for Ulva, and proceeded by the side of Loch-na-gaul. The hills continued to be covered with mist. In our passage by the side of the lake we [saw] a natural wall of basalt, of the thickness of two feet or more, both the surfaces of which nearly resembled a natural wall in regularity, but its form was not columnar.

July 23.—As the mist was exceedingly close we did not accompany our German friends to Staffa, who, however, set out with true German intrepidity, carrying a piper along with them, whose notes we heard long after they had ceased to be seen, and fortunately stumbled upon the island of Staffa, and with still greater good fortune stumbled upon the way back, though not without long and tedious deviation. The mist dispersing a little, I walked along the shore to a promontory to look for the blue or rather dark hills of Morven, of which we had had an imperfect view in our progress to Aros; but finding that they were completely intercepted, began to mineralise. The rocks are entirely composed of schistus and basalt.

July 24.—As the morning seemed to promise a clear day, we set out when the beams of the sun were beginning to break through the fog, sailed to the island of Ulva to take up our bagpiper, and soon beheld the white clouds of vapour rolling away in confusion and the lofty top of Benmore, apparently of a conical form, emerging amid broken and shattered columns, which seemed to tumble down his bare sides, glittering with micaceous schistus like silver. We saw the rocks of Ulva rising above each other in successive ranges of dark-coloured basalt. The shore of Mull to a considerable distance is exceedingly bold and steep, consisting likewise of irregular basaltic pillars covered at the foot by a waving line of silvery mist, streaked with the sunbeams, whence large flakes were continually ascending.

We soon passed Colonsay the little

and approached Staffa, which on the side of Ulva presents no extraordinary appearance. We landed at the Long Cave, through which we proceeded a considerable way, till the passage became very dark and extremely narrow. The range of basaltic columns on the left hand as you enter presents a very singular appearance. The columns near the top are bent precisely like the ribs of a vessel on the concave side; and where the concavity or segment of the curve terminates below, another segment commences, which exactly resembles the convex ribs of a vessel. The colours of the columns are gray, black, and dark brown. Some of them are black and scorched, almost approaching the nature of volcanic scoriæ, while at the same time they retain their form.

The island of Staffa consists of an immense pile of basaltic columns, the truncated extremities of which continue far beyond low-water mark. In some places they are quite erect, and these are generally covered at top with others of different dimensions, irregular and sloping. On the side of Tiree, immense pillars appear resting on a base of brown trapp. On the east side the columns are not so regular as on the south and west, but they contain numerous zeolites of different colours, chiefly green and white, sometimes crystallised and sometimes soft and striated like schorl, chalcedony, garnets, and martial jasper. We took some zeolites off the rocks, which nearly resembled a petrified cockle. The basaltic columns are generally of five and six sides, but they are frequently of four, seven, and eight sides, and sometimes of three. On the little rock, or rather island, of Boo-shalla, the columns are extremely perfect, and their truncated ends rise regularly above each other to the top like the steps of a stair. The rock is terminated by a few truncated columns.

The Cave of Fingal, termed in Gaelic An-ua-vine, or *the melodious cave*, is grand almost beyond imagination. The sides consist of immense upright ranges of reddish dark columns, and the roof, sloping to each side with considerable regularity, consists entirely of the truncated extremities of others. The bottom of the cave is always covered several fathoms deep with the waves, the roaring and dashing of which is awful, and has some resemblance to the low hollow tones of a prodigious organ. The roof is divided by a kind of regular ridge. The sides shelve down to the water with regular truncated columns, which form different rows of seats rising above each other, on which a powerful imagination may easily conceive an august assembly of sea-gods seated. The cave of the nymphs in Homer's *Odyssey* could never equal this. You enter an immense portal of black columns, which on both sides fold away with an air of rude grandeur. Their tops, or the solid part of the wall over the entrance, is covered with moss beautifully variegated, but chiefly yellow. After collecting various specimens and viewing the island on every side, we seated ourselves on a rock, and the piper playing a martial pibroch, we soon saw ourselves surrounded with sheep, cows, and among the rest of animals we saw three deer which had been placed on the island, and which seemed perfectly tame. This formed no bad illustration of the story of Orpheus. In Fingal's Cave the sound of the bagpipe, almost drowned by the roaring of the waves and the echo of the cave, exceeded in grandeur and wildness any union of sounds I ever heard. The island of Staffa rents for fourteen pounds, and is now only used for grazing cattle, though formerly it produced a considerable quantity of corn. One of our rowers assured us that in a storm the waves rise almost to the top of the basaltic columns and cover the whole island with foam. There is a tradition that formerly the island was three times as large, but being founded on columns, was undermined and sank in the waters. The sloping base of the columns on the west side, and the length of some of the caves, especially one on the west side termed the Boat's Cave, seems to have given origin to the idea. From Staffa we saw Coll and Tiree, besides numerous little islands. The view of the island from the sea on the west is grand and striking. The pillars of basalt tower majestically and seem to support the island, and the Cave of Fingal is full in view.

In a dead calm of the most sickening heat we rowed away for Iona, the aspect of which from Staffa is low and green, surmounted with white rocks. The Abbey appears in sight. As we approached we saw a number of swains and nymphs on the shore, neither beautiful nor elegant, instead of tending their flocks and herds, very busy making kelp. The town of Hi lies on the shore, and consists of a cluster of small irregular huts, the greater part of which, however, are much superior to the huts of Mull, and instead of being built of sods are composed of rough granite and porphyry. We visited the venerable ancient Abbey of Iona, the seat of learning in the dark ages, and the source of Scotish civilisation. The ruins are still sufficient to show its ancient grandeur. The greater part of the shell and many of the partition walls of the Abbey are still entire, and many of the inscriptions are very legible. The form of the characters on the tombstones and the flourishing of the borders, &c., are in a very fine taste; but the same cannot be said of the sculptured figures on the pilasters, &c., of the Abbey. In minute finishing and elegance of fritterwork, Melrose Abbey infinitely excels every ruin which I have seen. The windows of the Abbey of Iona are pretty entire, and the arches are chiefly of the sharp-pointed kind. The steeple tower is almost perfect, and displays a very elegant Gothic window, almost square, the interior part of which consists of a number of circular figures flourished diagonally. Various crosses exist in a state of perfection, covered with moss: their flourishing resembles that of the Runic pillars at Bew Castle. We visited likewise St Oran's Chapel and the Nunnery, the ruins of which are much less perfect than the Abbey, and saw the stones which are to hasten the end of the world. The small upper ones seem part of the handle of a cross. When the lower hollowed stone is worn out by turning them round, the end of the world is to ensue. At the door of the Abbey we saw another kind of font sunk in the ground, concerning which there is a tradition that whenever it is emptied of the rain water which it generally contains a northern breeze immediately springs up. I traversed these ruins with the most melancholy feelings, so great was the contrast of the ancient and modern state of the island of Iona. It is true the fishermen are industrious, which is more, perhaps, than can be said for the monks; but they preserved learning in the darkest age of the world, lived undisturbed in their sequestered territory, and introduced a mild religion among a barbarous race of men.

The regal tombs of the Scotish, Irish, and Norwegian princes are now incapable of being distinguished except by tradition: almost every ornament is effaced from their sepulchral stones. Some of the present stock of European sovereigns should visit Iona and pause a little on the confines of the other world.

I ascended Crachmore [? Dun-i] to have an idea of the island and view the rocks of which it is composed. The two extremities of the island rise in clusters of white rocks, which consist chiefly of trapp, gray granite schistus, and schorlaceous schistus. The low ground is fertile and well cultivated.

The island pays about £200 of yearly rent, and produces more grain than is sufficient for the inhabitants, who consist of 376 souls, according to the account of Mr MacLean the catechist, who accompanied us to the ruins, which he exhibits to strangers, detailing to them portions of the legend of St Columba.

From Iona we procured a boat to coast along the east shore of Mull, which we had not seen, and to carry us to Oban. Our boat was only a clumsy open coble rowed by four unskilful fishermen, with very awkward oars, over a space which none of them had traversed. But the most disagreeable circumstance was, that there was no room to lie, and hardly any to sit or stand. We coasted along the low shore of Ross, the rocks of which consist almost entirely of red and gray granite and porphyry. As it was high water we sailed through the narrow strait which they termed the Sound of Fechan, which is very shallow, and dry at the ebbing of the tide. The east shore of Mull is high, abrupt, and rocky, with a considerable surf breaking constantly on the shelves. In two or three places basaltic columns distinctly appeared, and there are some spots where the land is heaved and tossed like immense waves, and variegated with white rocks which have no inconsiderable resemblance to the Trosachs. Finding that our boat by some mistake had not been sufficiently victualled—as we had now the appearance of continuing all night at sea— we hove-to near Carsaig bay, and landed amid a strange cluster of rocks, where we found a hut and procured some goats' milk and goats'-milk cheese, but no bread. During the night the fishermen amused us with singing concerning Oscar MacOshin, who, as they translated the stanza, was so dreadfully gashed at the battle of Ben Eden that the cranes might have flown through him, yet he was cured by Fingal. The common phrase of making the sun and wind to shine through a person is nothing to this. They likewise related the story of MacPhail of Colonsay, with whom the Mermaid of the gulf of Corrivrekin fell in love; and snatching him down to her palace in Davie's locker, detained him for a long period, during which she bore him several children, and generally appeared to him in the form of a beautiful woman, advising him, however, to keep his distance whenever she assumed her fishy tail, lest she should devour him. But carrying him one day near the land, he sprang suddenly ashore and deserted his sea-goddess. This last story, however, seemed to amuse us much more than the fishermen, who appeared to be dreadfully afraid of some sea-spirit's appearance from some of the stormy recesses of the dark shore of Mull. I know not how far they might be to the taste of a sea-nymph, but I apprehend there was little danger of their being ravished by a land one.

About seven o'clock in the morning we reached Oban in safety, having experienced no real dangers, though we encountered numerous possible ones.

July 25.—Our German friends were preparing to set out for Dalmally at our arrival, along with Sir Francis D'Ivernois. We parted from them with considerable regret, after interchanging mutual promises of correspondence.

Baron Vincke, of Prussian Minden, possessed more intelligence than his countenance augured. With something extremely coarse in his features, and irresistibly laughable in all his gestures, he possessed the very essence of good humour, and extensive liberal views of men and manners. His attention was attracted by everything he saw or heard —the mineralogy, the agriculture, the quality of the soil, the manners of the people, with every useful institution. He was not a mere observer; he was anxious to transplant every institution into his own country, and always kept its improvement in view. He asked a great many questions in very bad English, and listened with great avidity while he smoked an immense pipe, which every person mistook for a pistol.

Mr Burgsdorff had travelled for three years over a considerable part of Europe to examine the state of the fine arts. He spoké most of the European languages, and had attended to the national manners and customs which he had seen. They impressed us with a very respectable idea of the state of society, the political regulations, and the respect for the laws in Prussia.

Of Sir Francis D'Ivernois we saw very little, and that little did not prepossess us highly in his favour. He seemed an enthusiast for the ancient French customs and manners, had the air of one of the French noblesse, and was, in short, a frenchified Swiss.

We remained at Oban all this day and examined the rocks in its neighbourhood, which consisted entirely of plum-pudding stone, granite, and schistus. We saw, however, some basalt, rolled upon the shore by the waves.

In the evening I ascended one of the eminences in the vicinity of the village to view the bay, which presented an appearance of uncommon beauty. Along the shore the sea was clear as a mirror, reflecting in an inverted position the houses of Oban, the ships in the bay, Dunolly Castle, and the adjacent rocks. At a considerable distance it was darkened by the black mountains of Morven, Mull, and the eminences of Kerrera. The intermediate space was beautifully variegated by numerous lines of coloured light, blending with each other in every possible gradation of shade, changing their hues continually as the long shadows of the hills varied their position. At one time the waves were crisped with long lines of red, purple, and yellow light; in a moment afterwards all motion had ceased, and the bay seemed one large still field of broken flaky ice. I contemplated this scene till every tint had died away, and, retiring with regret, composed the following Address to the ancient heroes of Morven.*

* The verses here referred to do not appear in the MS.

July 26.—This afternoon we walked along the shore to Easdale to see the slate quarries. The country presented much greater diversity of scenery than we expected. Soon after we left Oban we saw a small fresh-water lake on the left named   *   . Its situation, and the curves of the shore, might be rendered extremely romantic if the green declivities by which it is surrounded were covered with wood. We soon after crossed the river   *   , and turned down the side of Loch Fechan.

From the corner of a park of birch on the south side of this lake we beheld a scene of uncommon beauty, resembling in characteristic softness those which the lakes of Cumberland present, and perhaps inferior to none except Keswick and Grasmere. The sweep of the lake is large and ample, and its curvature

* Name omitted in MS.

doubles within view. The north end seems to stretch into a wild glen terminated by a rugged conical mountain. On the east appear a cluster of white hanging rocks, with an irregular wood rising up the declivity towards their base. The low hills on the opposite side are irregular and green. Small eminences, white rocks intermingled with clumps of trees and thickets, render the scene soft and romantic. The mouth of the lake even exceeded this in beauty, whitening in the setting sun. Crossing another range of high grounds, we passed along a small lake of fresh water to Clachan, and proceeded to Easdale, where we arrived in the dusk. During this walk we saw nothing new or singular among the rocks and strata which we were able to examine.

July 27.—I walked out in the morning to examine the small island opposite the inn, where the slate quarries have been exhausted. I was surprised to find every foot of ground in a state of high cultivation, and beds of potatoes at the bottom of open pits as well as on the surface, which vegetate amazingly in the warm soil produced by the crumbling schistus. At my return I found a card of invitation to breakfast from Mr Campbell, superintendent of the slate quarries, which we accepted, and were afterwards shown everything curious in the adjacent island, where the quarries are chiefly wrought at present. This is not at Easdale an occupation of difficulty and danger as in Cumberland, nor does it present anything romantic. The quarries are not wrought upon steep declivities but upon a flat surface. Three men commonly work abreast in a space of nine yards broad, and in a year generally quarry 120,000 slates, which are sold at thirty shillings per 1000, the one half of which accrues to the proprietor and the other to the labourer; so that every industrious labourer is able to clear about £30 per annum. About 200 persons are employed in these quarries. The slates are of two kinds—the whinstone and the coal slate. The first is of superior quality, but the last is easiest wrought. They are beautifully studded with cubic crystals of muriacite, so hard that the edges cut glass readily. These are sometimes prismatic and hexagonal.

From Easdale we took a boat to Loch Crinan, and rowed along a beautiful rocky shore indented with numerous bays. The sea was calm and serene. We passed through the midst of some herring busses that were proceeding to sea, and, coasting Scarba and Lunga,— the first a lofty romantic, the second a flat low island,—we touched at Resave to examine the rocks, which consisted chiefly of sandy schistus. We saw, very near us, the bleak mountains of Jura. The strait opened before us which is termed the Sound of Jura, lying between Jura and Scarba, and containing the dangerous whirlpool of Corrivrekin, with the distant view of which we were very much disappointed, as hardly any agitation of the surface was visible.

Loch Crinan now began to expand before us, and as we turned to enter it I saw an upright wall of basalt, standing alone like the fragment of a ruin, similar to that which I saw in Mull upon the shore of Loch-na-gaul. It had quite the appearance of an artificial structure from the horizontal position of the columns. Adjacent to it were various regular columns in an oblique position, seeming to have been thrown up violently through a chasm in the surrounding schistus, the sides of which were indurated and jagged where they touched the basalt. As we rowed round the outermost point of Loch Crinan I landed to examine the rocks, and saw various beds of trapp emerging through the chasms of the schistus, in one instance about an inch thick, and resembling in miniature the horizontal columns of basalt.

The view of Loch Crinan is extremely romantic, and the savage air is considerably softened by the green aspect of the adjoining vales and declivities. The Castle of Duntroon stands upon the north of the entrance, and the canal begins almost opposite to it on the south. We reached a pitiful inn about a mile from its commencement, and as I carried a few books under my arm and was partly dressed in sable, the landlady mistook me for an itinerant preacher, and the landlord, named

MacFadzean, an ugly fellow with a hypocritical face, immediately obtruded himself upon us, and maintaining his post obstinately, told me his wife wished to have a lecture. As I declined officiating in this capacity, I soon found that no provisions were to be got. So we proceeded along the canal almost nine miles farther to a pretty good inn upon Loch Gilpin, an arm of Loch Fyne. On our road we observed a considerable quantity of argillaceous schistus, gray granite, basalt, and nodules of basalt inclosed in strata of basalt decomposed. On some pieces of granite we perceived various streaks of asbestus. There is at the north end of the canal a shallow bason termed the Inner Loch, which at the ebbing of the tide is almost left without water. The ground adjacent spreads into a large level plain, which appears to be capable of high cultivation, and has probably formed in ancient times the bason of a large loch. From all this flat the sea might be excluded at very little expense.

A considerable part of the Crinan Canal is still unfinished. The locks to be employed are about fifteen in number, and their breadth is twenty-seven feet. The depth of the Canal is about twelve and a half feet. About 800 or 900 people have been frequently employed upon it, though at present there are not above 300. It has already cost about £110,000, and will require about £10,000 more. It is five years since it was begun, and it will probably be finished in another year.

The country adjacent to the canal seems very moorish, and we saw no good houses except the mansion of Oakfield, near Loch Gilpin.

July 28.—We had resolved to remain at Loch Gilpin-head to-day and see the environs, but at breakfast were unexpectedly alarmed by the approach of the Sheriff with the *posse comitatus*. As the Sheriff is an absolute monarch in his own district, we found ourselves obliged to cede the rooms we had occupied, and as they could no longer accommodate us, had resolved to retreat to another inn about two miles off, when we were relieved from our embarrassment by the politeness of Mr Campbell of Ashkenish, the Sheriff, who, learning that we were travellers, after a little conversation, with true Highland hospitality urged us to take up our residence at his seat, about six miles distant, on the side of Loch Fyne, named Loch Gair House. We accepted his offer, and walked over a wild bleak promontory to Loch Fyne, which we skirted till we reached Loch Gair House, a very elegant mansion. We were introduced to Mr Campbell's daughter, Mrs Jekyll, and the other ladies of the family, whom we found very agreeable. After dinner we walked up to the top of the rocky hills on the north of the house. The rocks presented nothing remarkable, consisting entirely of sandy granitine. The view of Loch Eyne was extremely beautiful, though intercepted long before it reached Inveraray. The elegant house of Lochgear presented itself, surrounded by trees at the top of a large bason of water, properly denominated Loch Gair, or the short loch. Loch Glaissean, a wild savage piece of fresh water about three miles in circuit, appeared beneath us on the moors. Loch Fyne, with its winding and indented shores stretching upwards towards Inveraray, uniting with Loch Gilpin at the termination of a dark promontory, was encompassed with dark heathy hills of a waving irregular outline.

Beyond Inveraray a chaos of mountain-tops presented itself; on the west the lofty mountains of Jura towered pre-eminent, while the rugged hills of Arran shut up the mouth of Loch Fyne.

I was here informed by Provost Campbell of Inveraray, and by a Miss Betty Campbell, that translations of the Poems of Ossian were first published by a Mr Wodrow of Isla,—a great mistake, as he only versified some of MacPherson's translations.

July 29.—On our return to Loch Gilpin from Loch Gair House we met Commissary Campbell of Ross, who invited us to visit his seat at Taynish. As this gave us an opportunity of seeing South Knapdale and Castle Swein, we accepted it with pleasure, and received from him a letter of introduction to Mrs Campbell. Retracing our steps along the canal, we entered a district which at first promised to be extremely rocky, mountainous, and wild, but which to our surprise we found well sheltered with wood, romantic, and highly cultivated. Ridges of potatoes appeared on the steepest eminences, and green streaks of corn emerged on the summits of the hills amid clusters of white rocks. Almost every spot of arable land appeared cultivated, even where no plough could possibly be employed. On enquiry we found that the spade was used in tillage where the country is very rocky and irregular.

Passing along the side of Loch Salenughellaghelly, a beautiful romantic arm of the sea, we reached Taynish. Taynish stands on a promontory between two lakes, the southern of which is termed Loch Swein, on the farthest bank of which are situated the ruins of Castle Swein, at four miles' distance. The house is of the uninteresting antique, having never been of great strength, and having lost all its ancient appendages by the present possessor preferring convenience to barbarous grandeur.

August 6.—At Taynish we found Mrs Campbell and her sister, Miss Lamont, ladies whose fascinating manners, good humour, and intelligent minds prevented us entirely from perceiving the lapse of time. Upon recollection, I therefore consider the period which elapsed between July 29 and August 6 as being annihilated; for certainly time passes at Taynish as imperceptibly as the magician of Skerr found it in the Celtic Hath-innis or the green isle of the blessed.

At Taynish we had an opportunity of hearing various species of Highland music performed with grace and execution on the harpsichord. The most characteristic airs which I have heard are Lochiel's and Duntroon's March. With respect to the latter, we heard various anecdotes while we remained in the vicinity of Loch Crinan, particularly a kind of unintelligible story about a piper of one of the hostile clans who was hanged by his friends for betraying them to the Campbells by playing this march. We wished to hear the Mach Lormondh March, but were disappointed. We made several cruises in Mr Campbell's wherry, while we remained at Taynish, to visit the most interesting places in the neighbourhood.

Dun Vourich, an old ruin almost totally defaced, stands almost opposite Taynish, in the promontory of Ross, on a high insulated rock. At the time of its erection it must have been a place of considerable strength, but, like most of the ancient castles, is commanded by the adjoining hills. It was a Danish fort, and tradition represents it as built by Murdoch, son of Sueno. The structure has originally consisted of two circular walls, the interior inclosing the habitation of the chieftain. The entrance winds in a serpentine direction within and without these walls.

Castle Sueno displays the remains of a solid massy edifice. It was one of the first strongholds of the Danes in this promontory. It seems to have originally consisted of an interior square, flanked with two round towers towards the sea and two square ones on the land side.

Beyond the promontory of Taynish the islands of Ulva and Dana extend in a right line. Both are very fertile in corn. The rocks are schistus and limestone. Beyond those lie various small rocky islands, used for grazing sheep and black cattle. We visited

Elen - mor - macoharmaig, formerly an appendage of the abbacy of Kilwinning, to which it was granted by the Lord of Arran and Knapdale.

We saw the ruins of the religious house on this island, which presented nothing remarkable except one tombstone, the sculptures of which were much defaced, and no vestiges of inscription could be traced. On the fragment of a cross, placed on the highest point of the island, there is an inscription in round Roman characters. We were prevented from deciphering it rather by the moss with which it was encrusted, and which we could not remove without injuring the characters, than by the obliteration. We learned from enquiry that both these monuments had been carried from Iona. We were told various legendary stories concerning them. The cross is said to have been conveyed as far as the Mull of

Kintyre by a vessel, which was unable to proceed farther till they had thrown it overboard; but the most remarkable circumstance was, that it contrived to find its way back to Elen-mor-macoharmaig in the manner of St Patrick's millstone.

Another miracle of this sacred island is a cave or cavern in the rock, or rather a large hole, into which the descent is extremely difficult, termed Macoharmaig's study. The Highlanders who frequent the island avoid entering it, as the legend asserts that whoever has this presumption is doomed to remain childless.

From Elen-mor-macoharmaig we had a near view of Jura, terminated on the one hand by Isla and on the other by the towering rugged mountain of Scarba.* In the middle tower the Paps of Jura, bleak and craggy, ex-

* See Note D, p. 282.

tremely precipitous near the top. The island of Jura appears to be one enormous gray rock, irregular and shelving in its outline, patched over with spots of black heath and dark green verdure. It grazes vast herds of black cattle, but produces very little corn. Kintyre at a great distance appears low and black, intercepted by the island of Gigha.

On our return up Loch Swein we looked into Rui Bhrettanich, an exceedingly good harbour between the islands of Ulva and Dana, which tradition reports was frequently used by the Danes.

The view of Taynish from Loch Swein is more romantic than from any other position, and might be admired were it not placed amid so many wild and interesting scenes.

The head of Loch Swein displays a scene uncommonly romantic and beautiful, hardly inferior in picturesque effect to the Trosachs, but which can only be viewed to advantage at several miles' distance. A similar cluster of jagged irregular hills appears, waving and undulating in their outline, now shelving gradually, now abrupt and precipitous, covered with * almost to the summits, interspersed with white projections of rock, diversified with light green patches of corn on the declivities and in the narrow winding vales. This scene of beauty is well contrasted with the bare rocky hills which skirt the loch and run down the promontory of Ross.

The rocks which we saw in the vicinity of Taynish were chiefly schistus, freestone, whinstone, granite quartz, and some steatite. Mr Campbell told me he had caused a search to be made for coal and minerals, but had only

* Word omitted in MS.

discovered what the miners termed a nest of lead, in its reguline form.

Mr Campbell showed me various copies of bonds of manrent and friendship, and of blood-acquittal, about the end of the sixteenth and the beginning of the seventeenth centuries, chiefly between the Campbells of Craignish and the MacRaws and MacGraws, and the Clan MacOharmaig or Shaw. They were tedious and formal, but conveyed a very clear idea of the barbarity of the times.

We left Taynish and proceeded to Prospect Hill, where we were obliged to remain this evening from the impossibility of procuring horses to Craignish. In the evening I called on Mr Gow, an agriculturist of great merit, placed here by Mr Malcolm to superintend an experimental farm, which I traversed in company with him, and had an excellent opportunity of observing the process of cultivating mossy land. This extensive flat consists of about 5000 acres, of which 3000 belong to Mr Malcolm, who has laid out 500 in an experimental farm which has succeeded to admiration. Within three years this whole champaign was an impassable morass, floated with water, covered with sedge, heath, and marshmallow, the surface entirely deformed and irregular from casting of peats from time immemorial. The moss is from four to twelve feet deep, immediately under which is a thin stratum of sand, beneath which is gravel full of water. The main trenches are from nine to eleven feet deep, and after the sinking of the moss require from two to four feet of additional depth. From these trenches gravel is procured for the formation of the traversing roads. In the main trench the water runs half a ton per minute. After draining the trenches, the irregular surface of the moss, covered with heath and marshmallow, is delved and levelled at the expense of £2, 13s. 4d. per acre. The covered trenches by which the main springs communicate with the principal trench are arched with the black bottom peat dried, which is insoluble in water. The first crop succeeds best in potatoes, by which the soil is greatly ameliorated, but even hardly produces its seed. Adjacent to the moss rises a knoll of excellent limestone, where Mr Gow intends to erect a kiln. From the difficulty of conveyance he chiefly uses shell-sand as yet, which answers extremely well. On about 200 acres of this moss there are at present luxuriant crops of corn, turnips, and potatoes; and the natives, who first regarded Mr Gow as a madman, begin now to view his progress with astonishment, but without abating one jot or tittle of their attachment to their most useless and most injurious usages.

Having procured horses in the evening, we set out by Kilmartine to view the remains of Carnassary Castle, founded by Bishop Carswell.* On our way we observed a Druidical circle consisting of thirteen stones, none of them very large, in a state of great perfection. Advancing, we saw by the roadside a very large tumulus or cromlech of small stones, many of which had been removed from one side and exposed the interior central vault, which I entered and found vaulted with large stones and terminated by a tall rough standing stone, like that which is frequently seen standing alone in fields. The vaulted chamber or pit in the centre of the tumulus is about the size of a large grave.

* John Carswell, Bishop of Argyle and the Isles, author of a Gaelic translation of Knox's *Liturgy* (Edin. 1567), the first book printed in that language.

Carnassary Castle displays great elegance of structure for the time of its erection. It is rather a strong house of defence than a castle, and combines elegance with strength better than any ruin I have seen. The finishing of the windows, the staircase, and various borders and cornices, are conceived with great happiness. I could not perceive any vestiges of inscription, but the evening was too far advanced when we viewed it. The common people still repeat proverbial distichs in Gaelic concerning Carswell, one of which appeared to be satirical, and was translated, " Was not Carswell a strong man who required five quarters of cloth to his hose, though he paid his labouring masons with a plack per day."

August 7.—I visited the ancient Castle of Duntroon this morning. It is a very clumsy, inelegant structure, and has been modernised by Mr Malcolm to very little advantage, as the walls, of seven feet in thickness, resist every attempt to alleviate the prison-like gloom which they throw around them. It stands upon a high rock upon Loch Crinan-side, and is defended towards the land by a strong courtyard.

Having procured a boat, we coasted directly to Oban without perceiving any object of importance except some very beautiful walls of horizontal basalt, between Easdale and Oban, which we had not hitherto had an opportunity of observing.

On the shores of Knapdale, Jura, and various parts of Argyleshire, the manufacture of kelp has been carried on to great advantage during the war with Spain. It is sold at present for twelve guineas per ton, but in time of peace it is only worth five, as it is almost superseded by the Spanish barilla.

The agriculture of lower Lorn is susceptible of very great improvement; much waste land might be cultivated at little expense, and very good corn land is barely scratched with the light trivial Scotish plough. In many places the distillation of whiskey presents an irresistible temptation to the poorer classes, as the boll of barley, which costs thirty shillings, produces by this process, when the whiskey is smuggled, between five and six guineas. This distillation has had the most ruinous effects in increasing the scarcity of grain last year, particularly in Isla and Tiree, where the people have subsisted chiefly on fish and potatoes.

Mr Campbell of Ross informed me that, when young, he recollected to have heard the poems of Ossian recited several successive evenings for several hours by some shepherds in Perthshire; but he did not remember the titles of the poems, nor could he say whether they had ever been translated.

To Dr R[obert] A[nderson].

OBAN, *August* 11, 1800.

DEAR SIR,—Here am I in great spirits, listening to the sound of a bagpipe and the dunning of some very alert Highlanders dancing the Highland Fling with great glee. Though I have acquired a few Gaelic words and phrases, I am really in considerable danger of mistaking the house where I write for the tower of Babel, for such a jargon of sounds as that produced by a riotous company bawling Gaelic songs and chattering something very like Billingsgate, blending with English oaths and the humstrum of a Highland bagpipe, seldom assails any ears but those of the damned. No doubt you will think this an agreeable variety after the uniformity of a college life, and, above all, an excellent situation for writing a letter. What, then, will you think when I inform you that I am just returned from Cruchan Ben, the highest mountain in Scotland except Ben Nevis, and have had an additional walk of fifteen miles between its base and Oban. In this country fifteen or twenty miles do not appear so long a space as between Dalkeith and Edinburgh. After returning from our Knapdale excursion, we spent the 8th in mineralising, with little success, among the neighbouring precipices, and particularly along the southern shore. At the foot of a very steep rock I stumbled upon the narrow entrance of a cave, into which I crept with some difficulty, as it was almost choked with long grass, and to my astonishment found a number of human bones scattered over its bottom. It occurred to us that this had probably been an ancient scene of massacre, and we dragged to light some of the bones which have long remained undisturbed in the grave. Groping round the dark sides of the cavern, it seemed to communicate with another dark pit of still greater extent; but as my ardour for exploring such subterraneous abodes had considerably abated at the sight of the dry bones, I quietly resigned the cave to its ancient possessors. Upon examining the exterior surface of the rock we observed two other communications a little higher in the declivity, from which we judged that it had more probably been a wolf's den.

About eight in the evening we set out in a chaise for Bunawe, or Tayniel, in order to visit Glenorchy. The mist began to creep down from the hills, and we were soon enclosed in a thick haze. Our driver, in order to elevate his spirits before setting out on the dreary road, had applied to whiskey, the universal medicine of the Highlanders, and not being extremely accurate in his calculation, had raised them considerably above par, and therefore amused himself by dismounting every gate which he encountered, and hurling them over the braes or into Loch Etive. However, we reached Bunawe in safety, and next morning breakfasted in Dalmally. The road from Bunawe to Dalmally, after crossing the rapid river Awe, proceeds along the foot of Cruchan Ben through Muckairn till it emerges on the side of Loch Awe from the pass termed Brander, when it winds round the north corner of the lake till it escapes into the strath of Glenorchy. The pass of Muckairn in savage nakedness and horrid grandeur even excels

Glen Croe; but the view from the water is superior to that from the road. It has the appearance of an immense rugged chasm. The west side of the foot of Cruchan Ben is shagged with trees, through which many gray points of rocks emerge, and amid which various cataracts are heard sounding, while the eye here and there distinguishes their foam through the intertwined branches of the trees. Near the entrance of the pass is a chain of waterfalls descending in succession from the brow of the mountain, roaring, foaming, and whitening, the effect of which is peculiarly beautiful. At the foot of the declivity the river Awe rushes darkly over a ragged bed of sharp-pointed stones. As you ascend, the stream gradually widens into a branch of Loch Awe, where the east bank becomes dreadfully steep and precipitous, or, rather, an entire wall of rocks—black, gray, and mossy—furrowed with torrents, that seem frequently to occupy the whole foot of the precipice, if we may judge from their tracks. At our return the west extremity seemed shut up with large dark clouds, in the middle of which was a large spot of sparkling red and purple, which in this romantic situation had a very picturesque effect. The top of this steep precipice was feathered with slender birch. At the entrance of the pass on the side of Bunawe we saw a vast number of cairns, which, we were told, covered the ancient MacGregors.

In the afternoon we left the inn at Dalmally and sallied out in quest of the smith, of whose family Faujas de St Fond has given a drawing. We found two brothers MacNabs at a village termed Barra Castle, whose ancestors have resided on the hill which they inhabit for the space of four hundred years, and have been the hereditary smiths of the Breadalbane family. They received us with great civility, showed us their lamp for burning wooden chips, and exhibited with triumph the coat of mail, helmet, and targe of their ancestors, which could hardly have been more rusty had they been buried with them. They were enthusiasts concerning the Fingalians, some of the vestiges of whose forts they affected to show us among their own huts. The degree of credit we attached to these representations is easily conceived. When we enquired concerning the Poems of Ossian they referred us to another brother, who resided in a farm about two miles' distance at the foot of the east hills. As my curiosity was now excited, I immediately set out for his residence, though it was late and began to rain violently. When I reached his farm, drenched to the skin, after wading through moss and moor, through long rank grass and tangled heath, I had the mortification to find that he had gone a little before to superintend his servants at a limekiln. Thither I immediately proceeded, when I found that he had gone considerably higher up the hill to the lime-quarry. Without being discouraged I ascended the hill to the quarry, but my Fingalian was not to be found. After stopping at the [quarry] till I was tired, I descended to the farm, where he had not returned; so that after waiting till it was quite dark, I made my way with great difficulty back to the inn of Dalmally. Next morning, with unabated ungratified curiosity, I returned to Barran, the residence of Mr MacNab, whom I found an intelligent respectable man, capable of detailing the information he possessed with considerable clearness and precision. He informed me that his ancestors had never possessed the Poems of Ossian, though they had always been acquainted with the characters there mentioned and the general outlines of the stories; but that he, induced by curiosity when very young, had procured copies of various poems, and had heard many more recited by the MacNicols, a family residing in a sequestered part of Glenlyon, whose situation had enabled them to preserve their ancient customs. Various persons of this family are still alive who are able to recite numerous poems of Ossian, &c.; and in the possession of one of them Mr MacNab declared that he had seen a MS. of at least thirty poems, but that upon enquiring after it lately he had not been able to procure it. He informed me he had given some poems to Dr Smith of Campbelton, but recollected the names of none but the *Fall of*

Tura, which he termed the destruction of the Fingalian women at Tayvaloch, near Glenelg. He stated that the business of his farm had so occupied his attention that he had no leisure to attend to these matters till very lately, but promised to collect all that he could in Glenorchy and transmit them to Edinburgh. He mentioned that he had seen a poem which accounted for the wars of Fingal in Ireland, without supposing him to be an Irishman.

Mr MacNab accompanied us to the ruins of Castle Caölchairn [Kilchurn], at the northern extremity of Loch Awe, which he informed me was originally erected by the lady of Sir Colin Campbell, and related a legend how Sir Colin, while residing in Italy, was informed by a brownie that his lady had converted the rents of Glenorchy into a heap of stones at the head of Loch Awe, and that, believing him dead, she intended immediately to marry another; and how Sir Colin returned on the marriage night in disguise, and receiving a cup of wine from the hand of his lady, discovered himself by returning the ring in the cup. The only ancient part of the building is a square tower, very much resembling that of St Rule at St Andrews. It was finished in 1440. The other three round towers and the interior square were erected by John, first Earl of Breadalbane, in 1693, for barracks. The square tower was damaged by lightning about thirty-two years ago, since which time the building has been suffered to decay, and is now little better than a mass of ruins.

We then took a boat and visited the ruins of Castle Fraoch Elan, situated upon a very romantic island in Loch Awe. It appears to have been a place of considerable strength, and occupies the top of the rock which forms the island entirely. The ruins are overshadowed and overgrown with trees, which descend down the steep rock quite to the edge of the water. Mr MacNab promised to send me a copy of a charter of Alexander III. granting this island and castle to one of the MacNaughtons, from whose descendant he had procured it.

We then proceeded to Inishail, another island, where there were the ruins of a nunnery and a chapel, which was a dependance of Inchaffray near Crieff. Here we saw various sculptured tombstones, in considerable preservation, chiefly belonging to the MacArthurs. One of them seemed to belong to the Lords of the Isles, by the insignia. On one of these stones we saw an inscription, not so much obliterated but it might be read by the help of glasses. I thought I could decipher some words, but am too well acquainted with the danger of mistake to trust a superficial glance of the naked eye.

At Glenorchy we likewise saw various curious tombstones, which seemed from the sculptures to belong to the Campbells and Sinclairs chiefly.

Mr MacNab informed me that his family were originally from Glendochart, but that the MacNabs, MacNaughtons, and some other clans had been ruined by adhering to the Baliol and the English interest in the time of Bruce.

He also repeated to me the history of the MacGregor proscription, which was occasioned by the chief's foster-brother, John Dhu, murdering the scholars of Dumbarton—the sons of the Scotish nobility—who had come, impelled by curiosity, to see the battle of the MacGregors and Colquhouns. The chief of the MacGregors made as many of these young men prisoners as possible, that having them in his power he might use the interest of their relations to screen himself from regal resentment. Having committed them to the care of his foster-brother, he enquired for them after the battle, upon which Black John drawing his dirk covered with blood, bade him ask that concerning them. MacGregor is said to have exclaimed immediately, "The MacGregors, that have so long been a clan, will be a clan no more." The quarrel between the MacGregors and Colquhouns is said to have originated from some of the former clan, on their return from Dumbarton, having killed and eaten a wedder belonging to some person of the latter clan. The MacGregors insisted it had been paid, which the Colquhouns denied; reprisals ensued, and the consequences are known.

Some of the MacGregors after their proscription being nearly overtaken by their pursuers, took shelter in a hut with a woman of their own clan. She, in the hearing of the pursuers, began to sing a song of triumph that her friends had escaped, and had already reached various glens which she particularised. Misled by this intelligence the pursuers advanced, and her friends escaped. Mr MacNab informed me that he had heard a song in praise of this action.

The beautiful air of *MacGregor a Ruaro* is a native melody of Glenlyon, where Ruaro lies.

The ferryman of Loch Awe at Inishail is in the twenty-first generation of his race that have served the MacConachies in that capacity during twenty generations.

Here we left Mr MacNab and sailed down Loch Awe till we came within three miles of Tayniel, where we slept last night.

Having armed myself this forenoon

with a hammer and a bottle of cider, I sallied out alone to ascend the steep lofty mountain of Cruchan Ben. The representations which I heard concerning its difficulty were extremely discouraging—indeed the people seemed to take a pleasure in deterring me; but my resolution was formed, and I quietly retraced my steps to the foot of the mountain and began to ascend with great energy.

In order to reach the greatest number of emerging strata, I ascended on the west side of a torrent that descends from the hill and has formed an enormous chasm in its side. The rocks were almost entirely gray and red granite, with a mixture of schistus, sandstone, and ironstone. During the ascent the chasm presented numerous cascades in the most picturesque situations. Both its sides are abrupt, ragged, and overhanging, winding round fractured and projecting points; sometimes almost closing over the dark stream, and immediately afterwards widening and expanding into basons which receive cascades of water. The rocks are sometimes covered with gray moss, sometimes of a dead black, fringed with birch, elder, and the mountain-ash, with red pendent berries, through which you perceive the foam of the waterfalls, which stun you with their mingling sounds of various degrees of deepness, while at intervals is heard the croak of the large raven. As you ascend you command a full view of the beautiful winding woody shores of Loch Awe and Loch Etive, the Sound of Mull, and the dark hills of Mull and Morven. The intermediate country consists of irregular ranges of brown hills covered loosely with birch, displaying in their recesses various wild moor-lakes glittering like silver in the sun.

As you ascend the hill divides into two peaks, of which the northern is the higher, joined by a narrow ridge bounded on one side by a steep precipice and on the other by a declivity little inferior to it, the passage between which considerably resembles walking along the ridge of a house. The top, and indeed the upper part of the hill, consists entirely of red and gray granite, but chiefly of red. The soil, in which some alpine plants and mosses grow with difficulty, seems to consist entirely of granite pulverised in the air. I collected some specimens of granite closely united with what seemed at first to be blue schistus, but which I apprehend to be fused granite. I saw likewise some blue whinstone near the top.

The stratification of the granite on the west side of the hill approaches regularity, and exhibits, over a large surface, an irregular rhomboidal division. No precise direction of the strata can be traced, but they seem to incline towards each other somewhat like the basaltic columns of Staffa.

The view from the top of the hill presents a scene of prodigious grandeur, and in my opinion much superior to the view from the top of Skiddaw or Ben Lomond. Hills of vast size appear piled on each other—torn, rent, and divided in every possible direction; sharp ridges appear crossing and mingling with each other, while their bare shelving sides, tinged of bright red and gray, are furrowed with torrents that seem to have burst from the sides of the hills and ploughed up their declivities to the bottom. In every vale is its own lake, winding along shelving shores and glimmering in the sun. Conic tops and channelled rough ridges were soaring above the white fleecy clouds that slowly sailed along their sides, upon which the shadows of the mountains lay like enormous branching trees. Above the rest of the hills Ben Nevis, Ben Lomond, and Ben Laoidh emerge with difficulty. A thin haze at a distance prevented the prospect from being so extensive as the height of the mountain would have admitted.

I descended over the enormous blocks of granite with considerably greater difficulty than I had clambered over them in my ascent, and, retracing my steps to Bunawe, pursued my way to Oban. I shall finish this letter by transcribing one of Mr MacNab's proverbs, for proverbs seem to comprehend the collective wisdom of the Celts :—

" Dh' fhéumaad oran bhi air a Dhianadh gu maith 's aimad fear millidh ata orra." " The original composers of songs should have been good, for a thousand have succeeded to injure their productions."

To Dr T[homas] B[rown].

OBAN, *August* 15, 1800.

DEAR SIR,—How eventful is the life of man in these western regions: one moment he is tossed by the most tremendous roaring waves; another, he is capering to the roaring of a bagpipe. A few nights ago we were dreadfully annoyed by a riotous company, who kept us awake the whole night; and only yesterday we were within an inch of entering the boat of ages and making a voyage to the green island of the blest. It must be owned we had no intention of making so long a voyage when we set out, and had so little humour for the journey that we were heartily glad to find that we had landed in Lismore rather than in the Celtic Hath-innis.

On the 13th we went to visit the site of the ancient Berigonium, and had a fine view of the castles of Dunolly and Dunstaffnage from the sea. Before us the rude towering hills of Benderaloch and Appin formed an excellent contrast to the green ridges of Lismore and Lochniel, the latter of which is shaded by romantic hanging woods. We entered a capacious bay, and ascended a rocky eminence to trace the ruins, which we were told still remained. Unfortunately our guide understood as little English as we did Gaelic, and we with much difficulty traced some remains of a rampart surrounding the eminence. We likewise saw the trench passing through a small moss between this eminence and the higher ground, where a water-pipe was lately discovered leading to the citadel. The eminence on which the citadel seems to have been founded consists chiefly of limestone and schistus intersected with bars of quartzose matter. About the middle of this eminence we found a considerable vein of pumice and vitreous scoriæ emerging through a chasm of the schistic matter, excessively indurated at the sides where it touched these scoriæ. The adjacent schistus induced us to think that this phenomenon was rather of volcanic origin than the effect of artificial vitrification. The scoriæ had a strong sulphuric smell, were frequently coloured green and gray and sometimes red, and contained masses of half-burnt limestone and indurated schistus.

Leaving Berigonium we proceeded towards Lismore, which we reached with much difficulty late in the evening, and immediately waited on the Rev. Mr MacNicol,* to whom we had procured

* See Note E, p. 283.

an introduction at Oban. We were received with the utmost frankness and hospitality, and parted with him next day, to return to Oban with considerable regret. We had not proceeded far from the shore when we were assailed by one of those violent squalls of wind and rain so frequent in these seas. Figure to yourself our situation, in a shallow open boat, navigated by ignorant sailors, who hardly understood a word of English; the waves heaving and foaming and dashing over us repeatedly, while we could not make ourselves understood, and could only understand the words "Cott tamm," bawled out at first, and gradually muttered in a lower and lower tone, till the mariners became entirely silent. After exhausting all my Gaelic, and assuring the sailors in English that they would soon drink salt water, I sat down very composedly on the stern and began to roar away "Lochaber no more," to the utter astonishment of the poor mariners, who verily believed they had got the devil on board. At last, by great good fortune, we ran back to Lismore, and returned to the hospitable Mr MacNicol, whom we left on the 15th, and proceeded with a fair wind to Oban.

Lismore, contrasted with the adjacent mountainous districts, seems much lower than we found it, yet it contains few eminences, and is little elevated above the level of the sea. The surface is almost entirely roughened over by low ragged beds of limestone, which assume the form of hillocks of stone, ruins, and often resemblance to the remains of an ancient churchyard at a distance. It is extremely fertile, as the land is low and sheltered and the soil warm. The rock is entirely of limestone, save where it is crossed with bars of trapp and quartz. Considerably above sea-mark there is a small vein of calcareous matter, containing numerous shells and bones of small animals about the size of a rat. Mr MacNicol showed us some horns of the bison and elk, and informed us that others of a much superior size had been dug up in the island. The church of Lismore consists of the chancel of the ancient cathedral, of which there are few remains. In the churchyard there are some sculptured gravestones of the flat species, but devoid of inscriptions; in some, the figures are elegant. Mr MacNicol informed me that the Gaelic traditions related that in the most ancient times a large block of oak was placed for a tombstone. One of these blocks I saw, partly covered with a flat stone. We saw the remains of a round tower, the walls of which are about twelve feet high. It is entirely round, and built without any lime or mortar, as far as I can judge. The interior part of the wall is supported by a kind of terrace, and about the same height there is a hollow way or vault about three feet high and two feet wide which runs round the building. The tower does not appear to have been ever much higher, and I cannot think that it has ever been covered.

As we were now within the precincts of Fingal's territories, and saw almost impending over us the black mountains of Lochgerloch and Morven, and as we resided with one of the most redoubted champions of Ossian, it must not be supposed that we neglected to enquire concerning the authenticity of the poems attributed to that ancient bard; and I must own I felt my incredulity melting away before the calm dispassionate conversation of the intelligent Mr MacNicol. The observations which I heard from him did not, however, differ essentially from the *Remarks* which he had formerly made on Johnson's *Tour;* but his local and personal knowledge gave them great weight. He told me he believed that the great texture of *Fingal* and *Temora* were taken from MacVurich's MSS., the existence of which he himself could testify, as many of those which MacPherson had left, and which have been published by Ronald MacDonald, passed through his hands. MacDonald informed him that he could hardly prevail upon MacVurich to show him these MSS., and only succeeded by promising to intercede for his lands with the Clanronald family. He informed me that many of the Gaelic poems in the possession of his brother had been published very inaccurately by Mr Hugh MacPherson in his *Conflicts of the Clans.* Mr MacNicol knew the Poems of Ossian before they were translated by Mr

MacPherson, and mentioned that Mr MacPherson had offered to show Mr MacLaggan of Blair Atholl his MSS., but that MacLaggan had failed in the appointment from accident. Mr MacPherson bound himself under a penalty of £50 to restore MacVurich his MSS., and on MacVurich prosecuting him for the restitution, MacPherson requested them to be allowed to remain a little longer to show some gentlemen, to which the other agreed.

Mr MacNicol, and also Mrs MacNicol, related many stories from the *Ur-sgeuls* which appear to be extremely numerous, and vie in ingenuity with the tales of the Arabs and Persians,—like which they are interspersed with numerous distichs in verse, which form the proverbs of the common people.

Fingal in these tales is represented as the man of smooth speech and fair countenance, who never fought in person except in some desperate extremity, and never till he had offered a ransom to prevent bloodshed. He is never conquered, though he sometimes encounters terrible dangers, and always displays consummate prudence and address.

Oscar is illustrious for his valour, but characterised by blind passion and fury. He first signalised his prowess at the battle of Ben Eden in Appin, in which, when the Fingalians had almost been worsted, the battle was retrieved by young Oscar, who had come from the women to assist them, brandishing an immense plank of oak.

Carril, the son of Fingal, excited the expectation that he would become the most formidable of the Fingalians. He quarrelled with Gaul about the marrowbones of venison, which that hero had the exclusive privilege of picking. Upon this the bone of a large deer was placed transversely in a wattled partition, and Carril tugged at the one end while Gaul held fast at the other. The victory accrued to Carril. Gaul had likewise the exclusive privilege of hanging his shield next to that of Fingal. Here Carril likewise encroached on his prerogative. A combat ensued, and Gaul, who was aware that his adversary could never be conquered except within sea-mark, confined all his endeavours to this point, to drive him within flood-mark, and succeeded by drowning his adversary.

Caolt was illustrious for his swiftness, and remarkable for his propensity to mischief. He overtook one of the men of Lochlin who came to insult the Fingalians, and fled so swiftly that his garment, which hung behind him, could never touch his heels. He entered the ship of Luno, and beat out the cold iron by his strength.

Ossian was the last of his race. Being present after the death of all his friends at the triumph expressed on account of a successful hunting match, he desired to be led to feel the deer which was killed, when he repeated a distich still proverbial, implying that the quarter of an elk in his days was equal to one of their modern deer. *Lòn*, which signifies an elk, is generally understood by the vulgar to signify a blackbird.

The two severest combats in which Fingal was engaged were one of them in Mull, where he attended the feast of a certain giant, during which he observed a black fellow heating a girdle for baking red-hot. A quarrel having occurred, the giant introduced a number of men at every whistle till he far outnumbered the Fingalians. As soon as Fingal began to fight, he found the hot girdle placed itself beneath his feet wherever he put them, which occasioned him to be terribly mauled.

The other time was when he happened to be separated from his companions at a great hunt with only six in his company, when he was encountered by six times the number of fair-haired men. After various conciliatory offers, none of which were accepted by his adversaries, Fingal enquired if his companions were willing to fight every man six. Oscar immediately undertook his number, declaring he had done more at the battle of Ben Eden; Fingal, who dreaded Gaul would refuse if left last, undertook that Gaul and himself would conquer six apiece of any race of heroes. The Fingalians were successful through the prowess of Oscar, or the valour of the last of Fingal's adversaries alone had conquered all the Fingalians.

On another occasion Fingal was invited to the feast of Magnus, king of Lochlin. Suspecting treachery he consulted his thumb, or, as another tradition has it, bit off a joint of his finger, when he found that if treachery was intended the warriors of Lochlin would demand their arms as they entered the hall of the feast, in which case he desired his heroes to retain their skein-fallan or side-dirks, and would likewise place two of the Lochlanach between every two of the Fingalians. These circumstances took place. At the feast Magnus demanded who had slain one of his heroes, who had fallen by the hand of Oscar. Oscar mildly replied that he would not deny that he had slain him, as fate or the chance of war had thrown him into his hand. The same question was put to Dermid, who, seeing that a quarrel was intended, fiercely replied that he had done it, and would answer the feud to all his friends. Magnus immediately desired his men to bind him, when the Fingalians rushed to arms, and Fingal demanded of Magnus where he had left his oaths [by which,] when conquered, he promised never more to attack the heroes of Morven. Magnus replied that he had left them where he found them. The combat began; the Fingalians were successful; and before they reached the door had slain three times their own number.

Connal, the Thersites of the Fingalians, excelled in arranging an army in battle array. He was a great churl, and made three resolutions which he carefully kept: 1, Never to see an open door without entering it; 2, Never to see a feast without partaking of it; 3, Never to see the landlord frown without giving him a box on the ear. Unfortunately one day he saw hell open, entered, and found the devil at a dinner, to which he set himself down without ceremony. The devil looked very surly, and Connal immediately gave him a box on the ear. I did not learn the issue of the business.

At our return from Lismore to Oban, I learned that a person of the name of MacPhie, from Mull, resides in a small island near Easdale, and works in the slate quarries, who can recite a great number of Ossian's poems, and that Mr Smith has derived from him several of those which he has published. I intended to have paid him a visit, but hearing that he could not speak English, my incapacity of understanding Gaelic deterred me.

After having fatigued you with so many Highland legends, I shall give you the substance of another Gaelic song, which was repeated by a boatman while he sailed along Loch Swein, and of which some fragments were waggishly translated by Commissary Uncle. The subject was the battle between Hector and Achilles. The battle was very obstinate, and Hector declared he would not resign his spear without brandishing it at his adversary, his broadsword without flourishing it over his head, nor his dirk without tickling his ribs with it. The song then proceeds to relate what an excellent dinner of fresh herrings they ate at the head of Loch Fyne after the battle was finished; and here I doubt not you will thank me for finishing this long epistle.

To J. R.

Oban, *August* 16, 1800.

Dear Sir,—Many persons are of opinion that travelling in an elbow-chair is not only the most pleasant mode of traversing a country—especially if it happen to be a rugged one—but the best for acquiring information. With respect to the degree of information I shall not pretend to decide; but of this there cannot remain a shadow of doubt, that it is prodigiously the best for filling a journal. I have travelled to-day since a very early hour, and have returned drenched with the rain and the dew, and after all I must own that I have seen very little. We set out in the morning to traverse the island of Kerrera, which belongs almost entirely to MacDougal of Lorn, or rather, if you prefer the modern title, of Dunolly. *Apropos* of MacDougal, I learned at Taynish that his family were in possession of the brooch which fixed the plaid of Robert Bruce, which tradition relates was thus acquired. The Lord of Lorn, assisted by the MacGregors, MacNaughtons, and MacNabs, defeated Robert Bruce between Tyndrum and Killin at Sayes, who narrowly escaped with only six of his companions. In the pursuit he was closely followed by the Lord of Lorn, chief of the MacDougals, when, turning short upon him, he knocked out his brains with a species of hammer, but was obliged, in order to extricate himself from the grasp of his antagonist, to leave his plaid and brooch behind him, which the other had strongly clenched while struggling in the agonies of death. Mr MacDougal, however, informed us that it had not been seen in his family for 150 years, having been lost in the ruins of the family mansion, which had been burned.

We walked round the island of Kerrera, which is about six miles in circumference, without seeing any singular phenomena. The rocks are chiefly plum-pudding; but we saw various bars of trapp and schistus graduating into basalt, as well as various masses of granite, reddish quartz, petrosilex, and freestone, some of which was much indurated and contained talc and schorls, some of which appeared to have suffered from fire. The island of Kerrera is covered with heath on the high grounds, and bears plentiful crops of grain, potatoes, &c., in the vales.

The harbour termed the Horse Shoe is deemed the safest in this country.

We examined the ruins of Castle Gylen, a fort belonging to the MacDougals, which was burned in a conflict of the clans by the MacLeans. It seems to have consisted of a square tower of considerable size and strength, as it stands upon a very high precipitous rock, which is fringed with ivy in a very picturesque manner, and is only accessible by a very narrow passage. The turrets of the corners are round. Over the gateway are three busts in the dress of Queen Mary's reign, with the figure of a bagpiper playing. There is likewise an inscription which, though covered with moss and lichen, seemed very legible; but we found it inaccessible without a ladder. The date seems to be 1587. The closeness of the mist obliged us to suspend our researches perhaps sooner than might otherwise have been the case, but not till we had surveyed the island with considerable accuracy.

I have been interrupted by Mr Stevenson, one of the principal inhabitants of this place, desiring me to preach to-morrow. As all my objections have been of no avail, I must bid you farewell, and proceed, contrary to the apostolical prescription, to take thought for to-morrow.

To Dr R[obert] A[nderson].

BALLAHULISH, *August* 20, 1800.

DEAR SIR,—When a man writes from the Highlands to a person who understands no Gaelic, perhaps it would be a judicious measure to write the names of the places whence he dates at the close rather than at the beginning of the letter, lest the reader should be deterred by the barbarous sound of the superscription. As I have some confidence in the strength of your curiosity, I shall proceed to the geography of the place, and inform you that I am now in Appin, in the ancient territory of the Stuarts—a name over which, ever in this country, the numerous Campbells have prevailed. As far as I can judge, however, the intrusion of this clan is not viewed with much complacency either in Appin, Glenorchy, or other glens which they did not originally possess. Almost every clan or name is supposed to have a specific character, which is commonly expressed in some proverbial distich. The Campbells are characterised as supple and insinuating; the MacDougals as useless to their friends and harmless to their foes—in the words of the famous Irish captain Alister MacDonald, who came to the assistance of Montrose; and the characteristic distich of the Cummings may be thus translated—

> "Guileful shall the Cummings be
> While the leaf falls from the tree."

The clan Campbell, which is not so ancient as some of the clans, particularly the MacGregors, was among the first which was civilised or departed from their ancient customs, as the Camerons seem to have been one of the last. Their influence was great at

Court, and soon became still greater in the West Highlands, till they are now more numerous, as well as more opulent, than almost any other clan.

On the 19th we left Oban and proceeded towards the Connal Ferry. The day was damp and dark. The mist prevented an extensive or accurate view, but presented a very picturesque phenomenon, stretching like a solid mass of snow along the low coast of Mull, and displaying a very strong contrast to the dark ridges of Benmore, which appeared far above it. We passed along the environs of Berigonium beneath a large hanging mass of plum-pudding stone, and traversed a low country to the Shian Ferry. The rocks were plum-pudding, schistus, and limestone. The high rugged hills of Appin were seen dimly through the mist, covered with heath and fringed with wood in their lower declivities.

The day lengthened as we entered the strath of Appin, a fertile romantic vale which extends along the foot of a range of very high mountains skirted with wood. We soon came in sight of Port Appin and reached Portnacroish. The great estuary which extends from Kerrera to Ballahulish is here termed Linnhe Lisach. Between Kerrera and Lismore it is termed Linnhe Kerrarach, while beneath Bals it is called Linnhe Shilach. Loch Shian is a branch of Linnhe Kerrarach. When we passed the ferry the day was dark and moist, but the view was extensive and displayed considerable variety, though not equal to that of Port Appin, which extends over the green island of Lismore to the dark hills of Mull, while on the sides it is bounded by the black rugged mountains of Morven and Kingerloch, Appin and Benderaloch. On the southeast, near Airds House, which we saw at a distance, the declivities near the shore are beautifully wooded. The old Castle of Appin, the ancient seat of the Stuarts of Appin, also Castle Stalker (which stands in a small island near the shore), concerning the age of which there is no tradition, has a very picturesque effect. We wound along the beautiful curving shore of Linnhe Lisach for about six miles, till we reached the house of the Rev. Mr MacColl. He informed us that a Mr MacKinnes stayed in his neighbourhood—a farmer by profession—who was able to repeat many of the poems of Ossian, and in particular some of both MacPherson's and Smith's collections. We were prevented from visiting him by finding that he understood no English. Mr MacColl accompanied us to a large pillar or single standing-stone in the midst of a field of corn. It had neither sculpture nor inscription, and he informed us that tradition reported it to have been erected over the grave of a Danish prince who fell in battle. It was dark a considerable time before we reached Ballahulish, and we scrambled along the sands of the lake to the inn, as the mountain torrents had torn up so much of the road that at last every vestige disappeared in the darkness. You fainthearted men of Edinburgh may perhaps look blue at this description, but in us it excited no alarm. Admire our courage when we inform you that we even plunged into these torrents themselves, and found—be not terrified—they reached no higher than our knee.

Next morning I walked up a short glen enclosed on three sides by mountains of stupendous * , which stretches directly to the hills from the mansion of Mr Stuart. The mountains

* Word omitted in MS.

on the south side are bleak, bare, and rocky, but on the north they are beautifully contrasted by a very steep hill of great height, which is nevertheless green almost to the very top. In this wild scene the appearance of the steep green mount was eminently beautiful and romantic, shaded lightly with wood and marked with the track of rivulets that have formerly furrowed its declivities. The tints of green likewise vary extremely, from the light green of the grass to the deep green of the fern and the dark green of the trees. This beautiful green hill is termed Beniveir, and its effect is much increased by the promixity of another craggy red hill with a conical top on the south. I then waited on Captain Stuart—a man of great intelligence and ardour of mind, with all the fire of an ancient chieftain—and was introduced to his family, where we spent the evening very pleasantly after returning from Glenco.

From Ballahulish we proceeded to the vale of Glenco, but our course was several times arrested by the mineralogy of the vicinity. A species of white sparry marble abounds in the neighbourhood, and is generally found in large blocks. The quarries of slate near the entrance of Glenco are intermixed and terminated by masses of limestone. The quarries are at present near the bottom of the hill, and the working is attended with little danger. The workmen are chiefly from Cumberland. The schistus contains numerous marcasites of a cubical figure, for the most part larger than those at Easdale. About a mile from Ballahulish is a rock which we were informed M. D'Arabien found more difficulty in reducing to any class than any he had seen in Europe or Asia. Mr H. pronounced it to be basalt, though it neither had the external appearance nor the internal characters of basalt, nor any tendency to the columnar form, though the rock presented the appearance of a regular steep wall near the sea. It appeared to me to be schistus which had acquired considerable hardness from having been subjected to a second fusion with quartz and talc. In this opinion I was confirmed by the appearance of a rock which we met soon after entering Glenco, where this fusion seemed to have been begun in some places but in many others was very imperfect, and various particles infused were visible surrounded by others which had evidently been in a state of fusion.

After passing the slate quarries we entered Glenco, and saw, by the side of the river, the ruins of the ancient mansion where MacDonald was murdered. The view at the entrance of Glenco is extremely sublime. The savage grandeur of the prodigious hills which encircle the valley impresses a degree of devotional feeling on the mind; but the scene is not dead and uniform, but pleases with its variety, though a person feels as if he were placed among the ruins of the world. Towards the north, the vast sheet of Linnhe Shilach winds along between the lofty ridges of Appin and Lochaber till it touches the bases of the Ardgowar and Kingerloch hills, when it turns gently towards the bay of Appin. Near Glenco it contains various islands, on one of which is a burying-place and the ruins of a church. The point of Lochaber is a gentle green declivity, and forms a beautiful contrast with the dark hills of Kingerloch, torn with chasms and gullies. Over one of these a stream of water precipitates itself into the lake, forming a succession of waterfalls and shingle in its course from the top of the hill to the bottom. Towards the south a succession of immense peaks and ridges present themselves, sometimes rugged with white rocks, sometimes covered with gray pebbles almost as thick as the sands of the sea. The morning had been thick and heavy, and the mist in immense flakes and columns rested by intervals on the summits of the mountains; but as they did not intercept our view, they only increased the sublimity of the scene. The entrance of Lochleven opened on the left, between ridges only inferior to those which enclosed the mouth of Glenco. The view on the side of Appin is likewise extremely sublime, displaying the green fairy hill above Ballahulish in contrast with a gray hill covered at the base with heath, but rising in a bare conical spire, and another naked red hill, the steep chasmy side of which has the appearance of a vast red ruptured crater. Advancing into the valley, a short glen shelves away towards the right from a steep green mountain, over a depression of the ridge of which the red conical top of the volcanic-like hill peeps in a very picturesque manner. The glen is terminated by the junction of this hill with another abrupt sloping ridge, rough and jagged on the top, and on the sides torn by red chasms. Now the scene opens in horrible magnificence, and the glen appears to be shut up by an immense precipice which is the entire side of a mountain of prodigious height, said to be more than 4000 feet.

"O tu severi relligio loci . . ."

The face of this perpendicular wall is honeycombed and scooped like the most beautiful fretwork of Gothic architecture, and presented itself to my mind, when I recollected the atheism of modern times, as the immense ruin of the inaccessible temple of the god of nature. This impression was strengthened by the view of a prodigious pillar of white flaky mist which seemed to descend from heaven and rested lightly on the summit. As we advanced our attention was attracted by a fine stream of water, which seemed to emerge from the bosom of the rock and precipitated itself with a murmuring noise in various successive cascades down a declivity in front of the immense precipice. At last we discovered a vast chasm which, during our approach, the projections of the rock had concealed. The light cloud of mist resting upon these projecting sides formed a stupendous vault of singular airy aspect, beneath which we could distinctly perceive the steep side of a more distant and more elevated mountain-spire rising in awful grandeur. We advanced still nearer to the precipice, from which we were separated by the rapid Co, when we perceived its shaggy side to be wet and drizzly, covered with black watery moss. Perhaps the aspect of this sublime rock could only be improved by incrusting its ragged surface with ice and icicles, when it would resemble one of the diamond palaces of the genii. Contrasted with this masterpiece of nature, the lofty shining rocks on the north, which shelve to an immense height with no great degree of declivity, lose their grandeur. We advanced to a small, black, round lake, where the Co has its source, round which we wound to examine the rocks more narrowly and ascend to the cascades. The rocks are chiefly whinstone and granite, which are highest among the rocks, and schistus, with a considerable quantity of quartz. We ascended a very steep declivity, passing by several cascades of considerable beauty, till we reached one of great magnificence, which is the highest, where the water shoots over a precipice about fifty feet perpendicular. This is superior to Scale Force, the finest cascade in Cumberland; but few persons will have courage to ascend to it. I ascended a considerable way beyond it to examine whether the mountain concealed any more cascades in its more elevated recesses, and beheld a scene of wildness and grandeur which excited emotions in my soul which I can never forget. I was alone, elevated at a vast height in a sublime mountain recess; immense piles of rock as regular as ruins surrounded me on every side except where I ascended; the winds of the mountain descended in hollow gusts, and a dull-sounding stream murmured sullenly by. Over my head the white cloud of mist formed a vast magnificent ceiling; some red deer appeared on the rocks above; and all around me lay strewed the blasted and withering birches of former times, that had fallen and were falling of extreme old age to the ground. I seemed to tread upon the heels of the old heroic times. "Lead me to the sound of my woods and the roar of my mountain streams; let the chase be heard on Cona, that I may think on the days of other years. The sons of the feeble hereafter will lift the voice on Cona, and looking up to the rocks say, 'Here Ossian dwelt.' They shall admire the chiefs of old and the race that are no more, while we ride on our clouds, on the wings of the roaring winds." Absorbed in these grand but melancholy recollections, I did not perceive the descent of the weeping mist till I felt myself thoroughly drenched, when I descended to my companions, who had suffered little, but had almost resigned me to the company of the ancient heroes. On our return, everything which was formerly so magnificent and grand looked dark and gloomy, and we had the satisfaction of beholding the terrors as well as the beauties of the vale.

On my return to the inn I enquired if the massacre of Glenco was deplored in any native Gaelic songs, and was informed by the landlord that he could repeat some on the subject; but unfortunately he did not understand English sufficiently to convey to me an idea of the texture of the composition, much less of its poetic beauties.

We made the usual enquiries at Captain Stuart concerning the authenticity of the Poems of Ossian, and were informed that numerous persons in Appin and Lochaber were still able to repeat them; and the Captain declared that he had frequently heard them himself. You will not be surprised that my scepticism is vanishing like the morning mist, and now it is extremely probable that my next epistle may contain an explicit recantation of my former infidelity.

To W[alter] S[cott].

Loch Moideart, Elan Shona, *August* 23, 1800.

Dear Sir,—It will probably surprise you exceedingly that a true son of the Church, who has imbibed with his mother's milk the highest relish for the severities of Presbyterianism and all the prejudices incident to that class of men, should have thought of visiting the Catholics of Moideart, those votaries of the courtesan of Babylon. Recollect, however, that the Catholic religion was never so favourably mentioned in some countries as at the present juncture. I myself have heard its fall deplored in the most august Assembly of our Church. It must indeed be confessed that the accounts we received of the manners of the people before we entered their district were very little calculated to obviate the ancient prejudices which might remain in my mind; but personal observation shows undeniably that they do not suffer upon a comparison with their Protestant neighbours, by whom they are misrepresented, and whom they in their turn likewise misrepresent. We had almost from the commencement of our journey been instructed to consider the *rough bounds* as impassable, and were disposed to apply to these districts those epithets which Mr Ramsay of Ochtertyre had lavished on the west coast of Scotland in general, when he advised us to substitute a voyage to Norway in the place of our proposed route, in imitation of an English gentleman who had unfortunately requested his advice when setting out upon a similar expedition. It was therefore with a considerable degree of hesitation that we despatched our luggage from Ballahulish to Fort William, and retraced our steps along Linnhe Shilach to *, a place which, to use an Irishism, we had only seen in the dark. We saw as we passed a considerable quantity of granite schistus and white marble in very large masses. From * we had a rough and tedious passage to Inversanda, at the foot of Glen Tarbet, where we only beheld a few wretched huts. Glen Tarbet is six Scotish miles in length, and is traversed by a good road compared with those which we afterwards met. The scene is wild and savage in an extreme degree. The hills which

* Name omitted in MS.

confine it laterally are rough, towering, and steep, containing in their bosoms numerous recesses or short glens which have no outlet, but are terminated by steep circular ranges. These commonly contain a rapid mountain stream, the track of which is very obvious when in rains and storms it is converted into an impetuous destructive torrent. They are termed *corri* in the language of the country. The hills display no traces of that soft green verdure which throws a shade of beauty over the rugged mountains of Appin, but are only gray with loose shining rocks and brown with long heath. A few stunted trees, half overturned by the furious blasts which sometimes rage in these glens, and the withered trunks of a still greater number lying on the ground, mark the site of an ancient forest that in the memory of the oldest men extended over all these hills. The rocks consisted chiefly of a species of granite containing a considerable quantity of mica and talc. This bleak, dreary, and uniform scene was at last relieved by the view of Loch Sunairt, winding in the sun among brown heathy hills, the bases of which were streaked with trees and verdure. These were the hills of Morven on the south end of Sunairt, and Ardnamurchan on the north. Sunairt is properly the name applied to the high district where the loch terminates, from which the promontory of Ardnamurchan, which is considerably lower, stretches far into the sea and almost covers the north coast of Mull. Strontian is the principal village of this district, and far exceeded my expectation, as it contains some very elegant houses which I did not hope to see in so wild a scene. It was late, and I had only time to call on my old acquaintance Mr Patience, settled a missionary in these districts, from whose local knowledge we derived much information. As the mines have been abandoned for a considerable period, the number of inhabitants has much decreased of late. The inn still retains the denomination of the London House, having been originally constructed of wood in that city and conveyed to Strontian in a ship. The accommodation is very bad, as may be expected. The floor of my bedroom was rotten and full of large holes, and I could hardly help fancying myself in one of those old enchanted castles where the miserable stranger was suddenly conveyed to some dreary dungeon by a trap-door. The panes of the window were shattered; and I discovered in the morning that an unlucky breeze had blown my night-cap from my head and scattered my clothes on the floor. After visiting the smelting-house at Strontian we set out in the morning to visit the mines, attended by Mr Patience and Mr Wilson, formerly an overseer, and a native of Alston Moor. The mines had been wrought to the depth of 100 fathoms, but most of the deep shafts are filled with water. The lead ore runs chiefly in a vein of ponderous spar of a dull white colour, though it is frequently contained in calcareous spar. As far as we could discover, the strontites is never stratified, but found in irregular parasitical masses, one of which we saw and traced in the rock. We saw three varieties of it—the green, the yellow, and the brown, in the last of which the striations are most imperfect. In the green they are most perfect; and the finest specimens of this kind have a greasy, unctuous appearance, and resemble very much the fracture of an animal bone, soft and porous about the joint. We saw likewise some very beautiful specimens of calcareous and siliceous spars, ponderous spar, and feltspar, termed by the miners chocolate spar.

The view of Strontian from the mines is extremely singular, and has the appearance of a colony planted in a very bleak desert. The long heath extends over almost every inch of uncultivated ground; yet scattered over it—between the village and the mines—above fifty huts remain, surrounded with patches of corn and potato beds, from which the people chiefly derive their sustenance.

After procuring a variety of specimens we passed over the ridge of the hill to another vein which had been tried. It runs in ponderous spar, and is crossed by several whin dykes and by a bar of black-jack about two feet broad. Descending on the other side of the hill by an irregular pathway, which hardly deserves so soft an appellation, while numerous withered roots and trunks of trees marked where an ancient forest had been, the bleak and dreary scene was softened by the view of the soft and pastoral Loch Shiel, one of the most picturesque of the mountain lakes. It runs between Sunairt and Moideart for a considerable number of miles, and communicates with Loch Moideart by a short stream. Its sides are green and fringed with wood, and form a very picturesque contrast to the bleak and wild scenes of Sunairt and Moideart. It is not equal in size to Loch Sunairt, but considerably exceeds it in beauty. Its effect on the mind is considerably increased by the surrounding scenery. At Pollock we were hospitably entertained by Mr Hope; and as the day was not very far advanced I resolved to ascend Ben

Rusepol, to have a more accurate idea of the relative position of the country and to examine the bed of stone which contains the garnet, having seen some beautiful specimens of this stone at Strontian which had been procured on this mountain. The rocks which I examined were uniformly granitous, but containing a very great proportion of mica in considerable masses and interspersed with numerous leaves of talc, sometimes of considerable size. The mass is soft and friable, and often intermixed with yellow veins of rotten stone, sandy and calcareous. In a vein of this kind, containing much talc and mica, the garnet is chiefly found. The view from the summit of the mountain, which is a ridge of about half a mile in length, is extremely wild and extensive, stretching on the south and west over Sunairt, Morven, Kingerloch, Mull, and Ardnamurchan; and on the north and east over Ardgower, Moideart, and part of Arisaig, beyond which appear the low land of Slate in Sky and the wild spiry and ragged hills of Sky and Rum, with the isle of Egg and its rock of prodigious size, which resembles in some degree the dome of an immense cathedral. Ardnamurchan is a long, flat, black promontory, and the most interesting object which it presented was the flat watery moss of Kintra, several miles in length, apparently capable of being improved. Moideart extends in two bare ridges, divided by Loch Moideart from the lofty hills in the interior part of the country. It is a bare uniform waste, spotted with gray rocks and blackened with heath. The surface is irregular and dimpled, but does not rise to considerable eminences. I lingered on the top so long that the darkness began to close imperceptibly round me, and instead of returning on my steps I chose what appeared to me to be a nearer way, and began to descend with celerity. My progress, however, was soon arrested by a tremendous range of precipices: to return was as bad as to proceed. I therefore determined on the latter, and the increasing gloom prevented me from perceiving my danger. Sliding cautiously down the wet and slippery crannies of the rocks, I at last reached the bottom of a precipice, the view of which, even through the darkness, made me shudder. But the danger did not terminate here, for a succession of others presented themselves; and it was with the utmost difficulty and fatigue that I at last reached a considerable cascade formed by a stream descending from the mountain. My situation here was wild and horrible. The winds, descending in gusts from the hill, agitated the tremulous leaves of the birch and mingled with the murmur of the waterfall, till I could have easily believed that I heard the still voices of the dead and saw the awful faces of other times looking upon me through the deep darkness. I scrambled for two hours among the rocks, the long heath, and moss intersected by gullies formed by the mountain torrents, and at last, almost contrary to my own expectation, arrived safe at Pollock, where I had been given up for lost.

Next day we crossed Loch Shiel and proceeded to Daliïie, the residence of Captain A. MacDonald. Our ferryman, a man of uncouth physiognomy, did not much prejudice us in favour of the Catholics of Moideart, and rather confirmed the account of them given by their neighbours of Sunairt; but they improved on acquaintance, and in Captain MacDonald we found a man of equal acuteness and information. His observations on the Highland character and antiquities were always ingenious, and for the most part well founded. He stated an opinion to which I am strongly inclined to yield my assent, though it is in direct opposition to that of Mr MacNicol of Lismore. The Highlanders, he conceives, while under the powerful influence of the Romish clergy, were neither so ignorant nor so disorderly as after the Reformation, while the state of religion was fluctuating and uncertain. The absence of Bishop Chisholm from Samlaman prevented me from seeing that gentleman, whom Captain MacDonald represented as well acquainted with many of the Ossianic originals. As we found it impossible to stay with Captain MacDonald, that gentleman accompanied us to Elan Shona, an island in the mouth of Loch Moideart, and the residence of Mr A. MacDonald. We took boat at Kinloch Moideart and proceeded down the estuary to Castle Tyrim, an ancient ruin of Danish origin, likewise situated on an island in the mouth of the lake. The ruins are of no determinate structure, following the windings of the rock. It was one of the strongholds of MacDonald of the Isles, and was demolished by the Covenanters. After spending this evening with my Catholic friends I shall know them better.

To W [ALTER] S [COTT].

GLENELG, ISLANDRIOCH, *August* 27, 1800.

DEAR SIR,—I shall, instead of throwing together a confused mass of observations, resume the account of my Catholic friends where I left off, and inform you that Mr A. MacDonald and family only confirmed the favourable opinion I had been induced to entertain of the inhabitants of that district.

Before leaving Elan Shona I ascended Penibhely early in the morning, the view from which is more extensive than could have been expected. The face of the sea was smooth and blue to an immense distance; the island of Coll partly emerged behind the promontory of Ardnamurchan; the isle of Muck green and interspersed with rocks; the romantic isle of Egg surrounded with a wall of rock, regular and lofty, and apparently divided in the middle, while both extremities are extremely elevated. Beyond it towered the bare, steep, peaked, and rugged hills of Rum, on the further side of which appears a part of the low isle of Canna. On the north-east, contending with the hills of Rum, the romantic and airy mountains of Sky, skirted with long lines of snowy mist, rise beyond the point of Slate, which is green and low. Then came the Sound of Sky, and

Arisaig, a country of brown and craggy eminences, interspersed with green spots, rising by successive gradations to a great height, while over the top of the depressions in the hills tower pre-eminent the black mountains of Morar. Between Arisaig and Moideart appeared Loch Ailort, a beautiful salt-water lake. Loch Moideart, with its winding banks, was glittering in the sun; a corner of Loch Shiel appeared beside the green woody hill of Torgallman, which rises abruptly from the moss of Kintra, and has, as I was informed, on its summit the remains of a vitrified fort. The view of Castle Tyrim was extremely beautiful. The appearance of Moideart is extremely bleak and desert: an irregular hilly country gray with rocks and brown with heath, rising into high mountains towards the interior part of the country. I was informed that at no distant period it was almost entirely covered with wood. Prince Charles, in 1745, landed in Loch Moideart, and stayed the first night after his arrival at Kinloch Moideart. He then proceeded to the head of Loch Shiel, where he was joined by Lochiel, and where the rebel standard was first raised.

From Elan Shona we proceeded in a boat to the isle of Egg, and immediately began our survey of that singular island. We landed hard by a small island, or rather insulated rock, composed entirely of basalt, and exhibiting some ranges of columns which possess a considerable degree of regularity. The rocks upon which we landed were likewise basaltic, but more irregular.

We first proceeded to examine the caves, which are only inferior to those of Staffa. Having procured candles, we began with the cave of the massacre, the most easterly of those on the south side of the island. The entrance is low, narrow, and irregular, and we were obliged to enter on all-fours. Before we could stand erect we found we were creeping over dead men's bones. The cave then becomes more spacious and lofty, but is still very jagged and irregular. It is formed in the basaltic rock. It extends in length about a hundred paces, and through its whole extent is strewed with bones. The traditionary account of the massacre is the following. MacLeod of Sky being injured by the islanders of Egg, sailed to that island with an armed force to make reprisals. The islanders betook themselves to this cave, which was unknown to their enemies. MacLeod, unable to discover any person, was withdrawing from the island, when he perceived a man standing upon one of the rocks, and pursued him to this cavern. The islander had the precaution to walk backwards, as it was a new-fallen snow; but this did not avail him. MacLeod demanded the aggressors to be delivered up, but the islanders refused to surrender them; upon which, taking advantage of a favourable wind, he collected a quantity of heath at the entrance, set fire to it, and stifled them with the smoke. We saw two other caves of considerable size, both formed in the basaltic rock. They are not quite so long as the cave of massacre, but light, and much more elevated. The first, only inferior in grandeur to Fingal's cave, though not regular, enters by a very lofty passage which, viewed from within, seems just half an arch. On the north side of the island there are likewise some caves, but of inferior note. The northern and southern extremities of the island are much more elevated than the middle, and both of them are enclosed towards the sea by perpendicular walls of basalt of great height, in which the regular columnar form is frequently very apparent. Between the bases of these walls and the sea extends a green declivity and flat, which seems to have been formed of the ruins of these walls, which have formerly extended nearer the sea. On the north side part of the wall is ready to be precipitated, being rent by chasms from the surface to an immense depth, and nearly undermined at the base, where between the strata of basalt a stratum of red indurated clay or ruddle appears. Over the whole surface of the island semicircular ranges of columns are perceptible, exposed in every direction. But the most remarkable rock in the whole island is that one of prodigious size termed Scouregg, not only for the regularity of the basaltic columns of which it is composed, but for the singularity of its form and the boldness of the precipice which it presents on every side except the western. We clambered up to the top of this rock, which consists entirely of the tops of clustered pillars of basalt, overgrown with gray moss. The prospect was prodigiously fine, though somewhat impeded by the haze which coloured the rays of the descending sun. Immediately under us lay the green flat isle of Muck, while at a considerable distance we observed the low isles of Coll and Tiree, with the black hills of Mull rising beyond the point of Ardnamurchan. On the west we seemed to touch the rough ridges and bare spires of Rum and the broken irregular tops of the mountains of Sky, while at a vast distance, almost on the horizon, we perceived the isles of Barra and Uist, beyond which the sun was setting, divided by a thin white cloud. The shores of Moideart, Arisaig, Morar, and Knoydart were full in our view, indented with estuaries and bays, on which the last beams of the sun rested, while their gray and lofty mountains presented a wild and singular horizon, that I several times mistook for hovering clouds of snow.

On the top of this rock we perceived the vestiges of a fortification, which seems to have defended every accessible part of the eminence; but the approaching darkness induced us to descend with celerity, and we reached Mr MacLean's manse after it had become somewhat late. The following day, though it detained us in the island, permitted us to resume our perambulations. We visited the south side of the precipice, which is of an awful and stupendous height, and attended more particularly to the mineralogy. The basaltic columns on Scouregg are only inferior in regularity and beauty to those of Staffa, and the triangular form is more frequent. They are generally smaller in diameter than those of that island, and are sometimes bent, generally in a convex form. The curve of the east side consists of two great strata of columns, dissimilar in size, the first of which is straight and perpendicular, while the lowest is bent and inclined by the pressure of a third stratum, which begins to emerge about the middle of that which is superincumbent. The appearance of the finest and highest columns from below is like a beautiful striated piece of strontites. On the south side the strata are more numerous, and in some places I counted no fewer than nine. The arrangement of these strata and the position of the columns vary extremely—from the perpendicular almost to the horizontal—through every degree of inclination. The ends of those which have the greatest degrees of inclination are often applied to the sides of those which are perpendicular. The inclining strata of columns are often separated by a stratum of perpendicular columns of larger size than the inclined. Almost round the rock the lowest strata have decayed, and present the lower extremities of columns irregularly truncated, while their tops, inclining inward, are buried in the solid rock. The basalt of Scouregg, and of the greater part of the strata in the island, is entirely different in appearance from that of Staffa, and, from the arrangement of its particles and colour, which is a deep vitreous black marked with red, may be compared to hematites. Specimens of jasper and agate have been found in it, and in many places the fracture and lustre are very similar. In the southern and northern walls which defend the island, though the tendency to the columnar form is obvious, it is seldom perfect. I observed, however, various clusters of perfect columns in both, particularly in the northern. The blackest and hardest basalt approaches nearest regularity. In some places it is extremely full of small zeolites, which are extremely hard and may often be mistaken for rock-crystal. In some places, where the form is definite and the diameter of the columns very great, they may be easily divided, and the divisions are likewise columnar.

Adjacent to the cave of massacre, and a little to the east, we found two veins of pitchstone, hard and black—apparently basalt impregnated with bitumen and mixed in some places with ironstone —running at the distance of about six yards from each other, winding and slanting, and generally about one and a half foot in diameter. At the harbour we perceived another vein of the same kind, but not so black as the former.

We regretted that our time did not allow us to explore the low island of Muck, the wild romantic Rum, nor Canna with its magnetic mountain. Mr MacLean informed me that in the latter island a tree was found in the middle of a plum-pudding stone. From description, the wood seems to have been charred. The attention we paid to the mineralogy and scenery of Egg prevented me from calling upon Mr Ronald MacDonald, editor of a volume of Gaelic poems. I am informed he has in his hands materials for a second volume, though they have never been published. The minister of Egg, besides the common qualifications of a clergyman, requires likewise to possess those of a mariner. The present incumbent is considered as a man of great abilities in his proper vocation, but excels in nautical skill every person in the Western Isles. His voice is tolerably rough and stern, and I believe he hands out either prayers or orders with considerable energy.

From Egg we set sail in a herring-smack, sailed along the bleak, bare, and rocky shore of Arisaig, till at last, weary with beating up and down under contrary winds, we landed on the green promontory of Slate, which, viewed from Egg and Moideart, seemed a flat, fertile, green district. We were entertained with great hospitality by Mr MacDonald of Tormor, who next day accompanied us to Glenelg. On our way we passed Armidale, a seat belonging to Lord MacDonald, and called transiently on Mr Martin MacPherson, minister of Slate. I regretted exceedingly that want of time obliged us to neglect our usual enquiries concerning

Ossian, where so much information might have been procured. At the bay of Elan Dermid, or Elan Oronsay, where there is a straggling village, we passed by the mouth of a cave which is supposed to be very extensive. The track of country over which we passed is so irregular and stony that it is necessary to use the spade instead of the plough in cultivation. The spade used is of a particular construction, and though it scratches lightly, turns over the surface of a great quantity of ground. The view of the distant hills of Sky—blue, steep, and rugged—is extremely picturesque, particularly the highest, termed Cuillean. From Elan Dermid we proceeded in a boat to Glenelg, where we arrived in the dusk, and find we have fallen plumb, like a covey of grouse, into the middle of a party of sportsmen, which consists of clergymen, seamen, and our hospitable landlord; and I have in the meantime seized some trifling pretext for leave of absence in order to escape from the surprising anecdotes, related with so much glee, of the sagacity of pointers—their passing along majestic as lions, their dead points, and many other circumstances too important to be thrown away on a person who is so little of a connoisseur as your humble servant.

To J. R.

FORT WILLIAM, *August* 30, 1800.

DEAR SIR,—Like the wandering knights in romance—who generally found a hospitable mansion situated in the most opportune position in the evening, though they were forced to wander all day long through the most dreary solitudes and frightful deserts—we have discovered a beautiful village by the side of a lake, which, after wandering so long in the wildest parts of the Highlands, we are very much disposed to call a town; and it is from this town that I have the honour of addressing you. And now that I have mentioned the castles of romance, you are not to suppose that it is deficient in point of a castle, though, as this is of no great altitude, I am rather disposed with the moderns to term it a fort. When we reached this town—fort, if you please—we had suffered nearly as much as the most disastrous knights-errant, not from the attacks of giants, dwarfs, or necromancers, but from the assault of a much more formidable adversary, ycleped *famine.* We have, however, contrived to demolish the enemy entirely, and left no vestige of him remaining but *the bare bones.* I shall therefore, without fear of molestation, proceed to narrate to you our adventures, from the time of our leaving Glenelg to our arrival at Fort William, in a country

> Where belly timber above ground
> Or under was not to be found.

After having seen the glen and the singular round turrets, which are more perfect in this valley than in almost any other quarter of the Highlands, we resisted even the temptation of a red-deer hunt, and, having procured a boat, sailed along the shore of Knoydart till we entered Loch Nevis. The vale of Glenelg displays a wild and romantic scene above Islandrioch. It is skirted on both sides by white craggy ridges, which at the head of the glen are crossed and terminated by a similar range of rocks. The river which flows through the vale is bordered by green meadows and yellow corn-fields. Beyond these the declivity is lightly sprinkled with shrubs and trees. The hill blackens as it ascends, till the heath mingles with the white rocks. Downward, the sound of Sky appears dark, wild, and picturesque, in which a number of vessels were riding, crossing and re-crossing each other; while beyond them towered in naked magnificence the blue mountains of Sky. But the objects most worthy the attention of a philosophical antiquary are the round turrets, built without lime or mortar. We visited and examined the remains of two of these edifices, and saw the site of a third, which we were informed had been demolished and the materials employed in building the barracks at Bernera. The round towers of Carron shared a similar fate. Both the towers which we visited are about the same dimensions with that of Lismore which we examined, being about 180 feet in circumference. In Lismore the wall was nearly of equal height in its whole extent, but in Glenelg one half is almost perfect and the other half is almost entirely demolished. The remaining semicircle is about thirty feet high, exceedingly firm and solid in its structure. The wall regularly and gradually contracts almost from the base to the top, yet neither this nor the partial demolition of the structure has in the least affected the remaining part of the wall. The thickness of the wall at the bottom is about twelve feet, but gradually decreases as it ascends. But in the middle of the wall there are a series of covered ways apparently unconnected, but rising above each other, and each of them surrounding the turret entirely. The undermost of these is about four feet high and two feet wide, but when nine or ten rise above each other the uppermost are extremely small. They communicate with the interior of the turret by oblong openings in the form of a window, which rise in regular succession above each other, diminishing gradually and corresponding in dimensions to their own concealed passages. Two of the ranges of openings or windows exist in the remains of these turrets. I cannot think their situation convenient for signal-towers, and rather imagine they were appropriated to some religious purpose. But every conjecture concerning them is vague, dark, and unsatisfactory. Mr Downie, minister of a neighbouring parish,—a man of coarse good sense but extremely indolent habits, a good shot, &c.,—informed me that in the neighbourhood resided one Macraw, an old man of one hundred years of age,—bedridden, deaf, and blind,—who frequently amuses himself with repeating Ossian's poems for whole days. Mr Downie added that he had heard him repeat many poems which have never been translated, and in particular a battle of the Fingalians in which cavalry were employed in passing a river. A gentleman of the name Macraw had taken down many of these.

Mr MacLeod of Islandrioch also mentioned that he had frequently heard Macaskill repeat the description of Cuchullin's chariot. This Macaskill, he said, went to America and died there many years ago. Mr Downie stated that many gentlemen of Inverness-shire had studied with great accuracy the grammatical analogies of Gaelic in its greatest purity who had taken no concern with the Gaelic Dictionary preparing chiefly by the ministers of Argyleshire and Perthshire.

The shore of Knoydart, along which we sailed, is wild and barren in an eminent degree. Indeed the range of coast between Glenelg and Ardnamurchan is extremely uniform in its aspect, and Morar is only distinguished by the superior height of its mountains. It is naked of trees, and consists of a vast sheet of heath spread over a great extent of rocky mountains and eminences, with their white points continually projecting without varying the scene essentially. As we entered Loch Nevis the scene was extremely rude and picturesque: projecting rocks and craggy isles threatened to shut up the entrance. As we advanced, the irregular rocks on each side, skirted with heath and covered with gray moss, began to tower in horrid magnificence, till we entered a capacious bason where the estuary through which we had passed expands into a grand extensive lake, on the side of which, lightly shaded with trees, we discovered Scothouse. Here we were hospitably entertained by Mr Gillespie, and took advantage of the presence of Mr MacDonell of Scothouse to enquire concerning the appearance of the country in the first half of the century. Instead of the savage naked appearance which it now presented, Knoydart was formerly clothed with extensive forests, and contained trees of very great magnitude. We learned that the ancient wicker houses of the Highlanders promoted in no inconsiderable degree the destruction of these forests. MacDonell of Glengary has constructed, on the side of Loch Nevis a little above Scothouse, a wicker house in the ancient manner, to serve as a hunting-box. The form of the house and the position of the rafters seem to be exactly imitated, and there is no ceiling but the roof. Instead, however, of forming the exterior walls with turf and sods, they have injudiciously covered it with slates, —an excellent idea for a virtuoso and antiquary. At Scothouse Loch Nevis expands into an ample bason, which seems to be entirely encompassed by the bleak circular range of hills in Knoydart and Morar, save at the entrance, where it likewise appears to be shut up by the wild and picturesque hills of Rum and Slate. The view of the lake here is exceedingly wild and romantic. The hills by which it is confined consist entirely of gray rocks and heath, skirted here and there with strips of thin wood where formerly flourished extensive and almost impenetrable forests. Beyond this range of the hills of Morar I was informed that there is a very fine fresh-water lake of considerable size, which we would fain have explored had our time permitted. From Scothouse we sailed up the romantic Loch Nevis, wondering how we should escape from the amphitheatre of hills, and, as we proceeded, continually baffled in our conjectures concerning the direction of the lake, till our progress was arrested by the tremendous ridge of Mainclach-aird. Here an amphitheatre of mountains, wild and rugged, whose bases are green, whose sides are covered with heath and whose tops are spiry and ridgy, shut up the head of Loch Nevis. We ascended by a winding irregular path into a mountainous pass which is as wild as Glenco, though it presents not such a tremendous front of precipice, and afterwards began to descend into a small dark vale of black heath, which is certainly as desolate a spot as can be conceived, and where the horrid solitude could only be increased by converting it into a valley of dry bones. The two passes into this horrid vale are blocked up by enormous precipices dreadfully rugged and gray, on the one side irregular and jagged, on the other one vast sheet of shelving rock, from top to bottom patched at intervals with black heath. These rocks are chiefly granitous, containing a great quantity of mica, but the precipices are often striated in large blocks like columns of basalt, and hardly more irregular. These are often intersected by beds of the soft gray stone which generally contains the garnet. Here I picked up a beautiful specimen of white spar studded with garnets; but as I was much fatigued with carrying those I had already collected, and had frequently deliberated with myself upon the propriety of tossing them all into the first lake which I saw, it was with much reluctance and hesitation that I preserved it.

We emerged from the vale of desolation into Glen Dessery—a green vale which skirts the bases of bleak and craggy mountains—where the prospect was only diversified by the opening of a corri at intervals, which exceeded the glen itself in savage wildness. From Scothouse we had brought some provisions with us, and determined as fast as possible to alleviate ourselves of the weight of them. There was no hut in view, and we seated ourselves in the true pilgrim style by the side of a cool mountain rivulet, and, producing our provisions, made a very hearty meal, which was interrupted by a Highlander joining us who could only speak Gaelic. Resuming our journey, we reached Loch Arkeig before evening, and had a fine view of one of the wildest fresh-water lakes I ever saw. Loch Arkeig is wild and savage, but has little in common with Loch Nevis, that overawes the mind by the immense rocks and mountains which enclose it on every side. The wildness of Loch Arkeig, after the awful scenes through which we had passed, seemed more akin to beauty; and yet I sincerely believe it was neither beautiful nor picturesque if compared with Loch Lomond or Loch Ketterin. Loch Arkeig winds along between two ridges of hills, covered with heath but not interrupted by rocks; of considerable height, but rather declining than abrupt. It is eighteen miles long, and never above two in breadth. The sides of the lake are fringed with wood. Near its termination it loses from this circumstance much of its wildness, and becomes picturesque and beautiful, particularly about [Auchnacarrie], the seat of Lochiel. Next morning we very injudiciously crossed the hills between Loch Arkeig and Loch-Eil, instead of sailing to the foot of Loch Arkeig. The seat was bleak, heathy, and barren, but too uniform to divert our attention from the most frightful ground for walking that we had met. Extensive barren glens opened upon us at intervals; and we saw one fine mountain cataract, superior to a very fine one at the head of Loch Nevis and equal to the one we observed in Glenelg. The view of Loch-Eil through the opening of the hills at Fassefern is extremely beautiful, especially when contrasted with the bleak uninteresting scene through which we had passed. Loch-Eil is much softer in its general effect than Loch Arkeig; the hills are not so high, their bases are green, and there are various clusters of villages upon its banks, as well as some elegant seats towards Fort William. The view of the gigantic Ben Nevis, streaked on the top with snow, towering over Fort William, is exceedingly grand; and when the eye descends to the vale, it rests on the ruins of Inverlochy Castle. We sailed down Loch-Eil till we reached the great curve which it makes before it reaches Fort William, when our eyes were agreeably relieved by the view of an elegant village, much superior to Oban in regularity and beauty. It contains about 1600 inhabitants, and is at present named Gordonsburgh, but was formerly denominated Maryborough till it was reclaimed by the Duke of Gordon, not long ago. The view of Gordonsburgh, in such a wild and romantic situation, afforded uncommon pleasure, as we had feasted to satiety upon the most rugged and uncultivated scenes in nature. The appearance of Fort William is very unwarlike, being situated extremely low and commanded by numerous eminences in the vicinity. Indeed, as I approached, I mistook the ruins of Inverlochy for that famed fortress which defied all the attempts of the Highlanders in 1745. After being accustomed for a fortnight to trust to Providence almost entirely for our daily food as well as lodging, I shall enjoy with tolerable relish the comforts of a tolerable inn. As I have just procured a book of Gaelic songs, my curiosity excites me to terminate this long epistle and make another effort to acquire a little of that language, the knowledge of which is equally necessary and difficult.

To Dr R[obert] A[nderson].

INVERNESS, *September* 3, 1800.

DEAR SIR,—After a life of danger, difficulty, and everything but despair for more than a fortnight, I have arrived safe in the northern capital. I could detail to you a tissue of adventures as wonderful as those of the most renowned knight-errants, and as fabulous too; but as my design is rather to inform your judgment than astonish your imagination, I shall confine myself to the mere detail of events as they occurred. The next morning after our arrival at Fort William (August 31), having provided a guide, we began to ascend Ben Nevis by a route which seemed winding and circuitous. Soon after we entered Glen Nevis we began to ascend gradually, winding along the foot of the mountain till we reached a gully of considerable depth, after passing a slender wood of birch. Ascending the gully, we began to climb a steep heathy declivity, shaping our course in a zigzag direction. The heath became more and more stunted as we proceeded, and at last we found nothing but yellow moss and gray stones, which occupied the whole side of the mountain and rendered it exceedingly difficult to advance. The day, which was at first remarkably fine, became now dull and leaden; and when we reached the top we found the view not only very circumscribed, but almost entirely divested of magnificence and grandeur. On the north side, Ben Nevis is steep but not precipitous; on the south, it is a vast, ragged, and uneven precipice, the height of which in some places is represented to be 500 yards. This precipice consists entirely of granite, which in numerous places has the appearance of regular strata, and is divided into blocks and slabs, generally of a rhombic form. The top of the hill is entirely covered with loose slabs and masses of the same substance, which, from the exterior, one would take to be slag. A few masses of vitrified slag, small and loose likewise, presented themselves, as well as various pieces of plum-pudding stone. The enormous precipice on the south side seems to have been formed in the same manner as the east side of Skiddaw, by rending obliquely from the hill those enormous mountainous ridges on the south which are connected with the principal eminence, and little inferior to it in height. On the top of the hill, as well as in the chasms of the precipice, the snow lies unmelted through the whole summer, and this singularity very soon produced a match of snowballs. The top of the mountain is of considerable extent, and entirely covered with loose stones, chiefly granitine. The view from the mountain is extremely extensive, but by no means so grand as that from Cruchan Ben, as the subjacent country lies not in such wild and terrific disorder. From the one you see nothing but sharp ridges and peaks and narrow valleys; from the other you overlook, indeed, numerous mountains, and see ridge rising behind ridge, but they are more distant, and the adjacent flat ground is more extensive.

After we had remained about two hours on the mountain, and there was no hope of the day becoming more favourable, we began to descend. A considerable way down, the prospect began to open a little and the day to become more cheerful; and while hesitating whether to return or not, we were joined by a party ascending. I returned with them, and had some favourable glimpses; but the chief object I saw was a cataract near the head of Glen Nevis, little if at all inferior to the Fall of Eyres. The increasing mist prevented me from viewing it nearer. The large white columns of mist rested on the tops of the hills, and though they precluded an extensive view, except by glimpses, they added to the sublimity of the scene.

The gentlemen whom I returned with

were Cameron of Glen Nevis, his brother, and cousin, Captain Cameron, and a Mr Grant from Glen Urquhart, who came up the hill, almost exhausted, long after the others. He plied the whiskey bottle with considerable alacrity, but notwithstanding, found the descent more perilous and difficult than the ascent. After descending over the rough rolling stones to the steep heathy declivity, we all assembled at a well, and began to drink lustily. Here Mr Grant's courage entirely failed; and he protested that he would move no further, exclaiming that it was utterly impossible to conceive what could have induced him to ascend Ben Nevis had he not been entirely forsaken by Providence, and imprecating every curse on his head if he was ever again found on this mountain. Captain Cameron and I desired him to take hold of us firmly and we would soon whisk him to the bottom, but he assured us he preferred being upon his *own parole*. Ben Nevis is 4370 feet high.

Next day we left Fort William, and proceeded by the ruins of Inverlochy Castle towards Highbridge. These ruins are considerably perfect, and display the style of building. The form is that of a central square flanked with round towers. Inveraray Castle is said to have been built after this model. We likewise passed within a short distance of Lochaber, whence the district derives its appellation, which had been pointed out to us from Ben Nevis, but was so small that we could hardly distinguish it. At Highbridge we passed the deep rapid river Spean, and proceeded through a bleak, heathy, uninteresting district to Keppoch, till lately the residence of a family of MacDonells, introduced about 400 years ago by Mackintosh of that Ilk to oppose the

Camerons his neighbours, by whose incursions he was frequently harassed. The MacDonells of Keppoch not only maintained themselves against the Camerons, but against Mackintosh their superior, whom they encountered and defeated in one of the last skirmishes of the clans; and without possessing a foot of allodial territory, the chief was able to vie with his most powerful neighbours in the number of his retainers. The district between Fort William and Glen Roy is a dark heathy flat. The neighbouring hills are of considerable height, but seem diminished by the contrast which they form to Ben Nevis. We advanced to some green rising grounds which shut up the entrance into Glen Roy, and soon saw the vestiges of the Parallel Roads winding round the receding ridges, which form the valley as they separate from each other at the entrance. As we advanced, a romantic and beautiful valley of considerable extent opened upon us. The two ridges or lines of hills by which it was enclosed were white and craggy at the top, brown and heathy in the middle, and green at the base, where light fringes of wood extended themselves in irregular strips on the banks of the rivulet denominated Ruagh, or the *red*, whence the valley derives its name. On the heathy declivities of these ridges, and near the middle of their height, the Parallel Roads appear—three in number—on each side of the valley. The respective parallels on the one side are upon the same level with those on the other; but the distance of the different parallels from each other is not equal, as the midmost and highest are much farther distant than the former and the lowest. Where the outline of the declivity from any considerable gully or projection fluctuates, the winding parallels partake of the irregularity; but where an inconsiderable gully has been formed by a torrent, they are interrupted. The roads are therefore of posterior formation to the first, but of prior antiquity to the latter.

These roads have been awkwardly enough adduced as proofs of an early civilisation of the Highlands; but it would certainly have been more convenient to have constructed roads through districts devoid of them, than to have formed six in one small valley. Some have supposed that they have been formed by successive depressions of a lake which formerly occupied the whole valley. Not only are the passes or entrances of the glen at both extremities averse to this supposition— as they are both irregular, the ridges receding or folding away from each other—but other circumstances render it impossible. The level is not always accurately preserved through the whole extent of the same parallel, especially in the middle one on the south side; neither are all the parallels beneath the level of the lateral communications with the valley through the partial depressions of the confining ridges. A more probable opinion is, that they were formed for the convenience of hunting when the Scotish court resided at Inverlochy, and the whole glen was a royal forest, as tradition reports. These roads extend between six and eight miles up the glen, when they vanish entirely on the one side, and only two appear on the other. We were informed that they occur likewise in two small adjacent glens, as well as in Glenorchy, near Dalmally. The roads in Glen Roy are about thirty feet in breadth, and appear to have been formed with great care, as the intercepted declivity between the parallels seems to have been smoothed away, so that the earth falling down might never obstruct the road. I dug away the surface in various places to ascertain whether they had been paved, and am induced to think that they were paved very skilfully.

As we proceeded leisurely to examine the Parallel Roads, it was dark before we reached a miserable inn, where we could procure no species of accommodation. The view of the valley by moonlight was even more picturesque than during the day, and its harshest aspects were softened by the pale yellow lustre which floated lightly down the declivities and rested on the stream of the valley. But as we were very much fatigued, we were terribly disconcerted by learning at the inn that they had not a particle of bread, and had just finished all the potatoes which were dug. We set out early in the morning, expecting to reach some place where provisions might be procured; but after travelling ten miles through a wild strath covered with heath and rushes, we saw only some wretched huts, which were confessedly inferior to any we had hitherto seen. We saw one, of green sods, which a man might have easily leaped over, the entrance of which was not above three feet high, without any door; yet in this wretched hovel we found a woman and some children. At the head of this glen, after fasting twenty-nine hours, in a transport of rage I resolved to adopt the resolutions of Conan the Fingalian, regardless of all consequences. We therefore rushed without ceremony into the first open door we found, but as no person was at meat, we had no opportunity of putting in practice the most dangerous part of the system. Indeed the first experiment would probably have been extremely unfortunate, as the hut was completely filled with stout Highlanders. Having, however, procured three horses,—for we were still fourteen miles from Fort Augustus,—we proceeded towards the steep, bleak, rocky pass of Corryarrick, and ascended the zigzag, which I cannot think above a mile in length. The side of the mountain is indeed steep, bleak, and dismal, but neither great nor sublime. The soil over which the road passes along the declivity is wet and plashy, abounding in springs and void of canals or drains, which ought to have been formed in constructing the road. Near the top of the mountain it is not entirely covered with heath, but many spaces appear of a bare whitish surface, watery and full of loose stones. The day was extremely fine, but the view from Corryarrick was neither great, beautiful, nor picturesque. On the south it looked into the wild black region of Badenoch, surmounting the heathy hills which separate it from the similar district of Lochaber; on the west and north it extended from Ben Nevis over the hills of Lochaber, Glenelg, and Kintail to the gray heathy mountains on the confines of Ross; but the scene was neither diversified by variety nor striking from its native grandeur.

As we descended a gradual declivity of considerable extent, the most beautiful object which presented itself was Loch Gary, winding round a green promontory covered with wood. After passing a small lake we arrived at Fort Augustus, termed in Gaelic Kil-y-a-Cumming, the burial-place of the Cummings. Fort Augustus is situated on the western extremity of Loch Ness, in the district of Abertarff, between the rivers Tarff and Oich. It is rather an elegant village than a town, but the buildings are extremely neat. The fort consists of a great square flanked with bastions. It is of no strength either from the works—which are very trifling—or from the situation, being commanded by numerous heights in the vicinity.

From Fort Augustus we proceeded towards Strath Errick, and ascended a gray rocky ridge which overhangs the fort, whence we had a glance of the green woody opening of Glen Morrison on the opposite side of Loch Ness, the view of which was soon interrupted. The country grew bleak and desert without becoming picturesque or romantic. As we advanced the scenery improved. The general aspect remained wild and barren, consisting of short heath strewed thick with gray stones;

but it was softened by the view of yellow corn-fields and three small moor-lakes lightly fringed with wood, and by a glimpse of Loch Ness between the rugged rocks, with green trees climbing the white and craggy eminences on the opposite side. Before the Fall of Fyres, Strath Errick becomes eminently beautiful and picturesque. The road winds beneath some fine hanging trees, and reaches a bridge thrown over a narrow chasm, where the stream falls with great violence over a precipice above twenty feet in height, forming a beautiful cascade. As you look up the river you view a most enchanting scene, which combines on a small scale numerous beauties. Above the cascade is a fine green plain nearly circular in form. On the right hand it is bounded by an irregular wall of loose hanging precipices, while on the left a light wood of birches, through which the heath of the soil appears, forms an agreeable contrast. You descend by the side of a horrid chasm, with the beautiful banks of Loch Ness full in view, shaded with wood and surmounted by heath and rocks, till, directing your eye as the stunning noise directs, through the loose overhanging birches you perceive the river precipitating itself through a narrow chasm of broken rocks in a white continuous stream into an abyss of which you cannot see the bottom. Scrambling down a steep irregular path, you perceive the water fall more and more distinctly, till you reach a green projecting bank, where you have a perfect view of both the cascade and bason. The cascade, or fall, seems to be prodigiously magnified in the relations of travellers. Instead of 470 feet perpendicular, it did not appear to me that the water could ever fall above 150 feet. The bason is nearly of a circular shape, and forms only a small part of a vast circular gulf which extends considerably beneath it, and seems to have been made by the cataract in its progress to its present station. The precipices which enclose the gulf are everywhere bristled over and darkened with trees, which are chiefly the birch and mountain-ash. The rock on the south side is in many places covered with ivy and young oaks. The appearance of the trees, seen through the narrow chasm by which the river precipitates its waters, is extremely picturesque. The green bank is covered with spray when the cataract is full of water, and shakes perceptibly by the violence of the fall and the impetus of the stream. When the river is swollen, the fall is surveyed at greatest advantage from the lower verge of the circular bank, which likewise combines a view of the House of Fyres.

We left the Fall of Fyres and proceeded

to the General's Hut,* a wretched inn. A little beyond the General's Hut the beautiful romantic valley of Urquhart burst upon the eye, where the picturesque ruin of Castle Urquhart projects into Loch Ness. The scene is uncommonly sweet; and judging by its appearance from the opposite side of the lake, I am inclined to think that it resembles considerably the soft pastoral valley of Grasmere. The flat seemed to consist of green meadows and yellow corn-fields. The declivity was shaded with wood, while the tops of the hill were craggy and bleak, especially Mealfourvounie, which divides Urquhart from Glen Morrison. We experienced a terrible disappointment here when we found that no boat could be procured to ferry us over to

* So termed from having been for a time the residence of General Wade, while constructing the military roads in the Highlands in 1726.

Urquhart; and I hardly know if we derived any consolation from being informed that the dead swell of the waves was so great that no boat could possibly venture on the lake. Conceiving it therefore to be fruitless to make any further attempts to procure a boat, we proceeded without further delay towards Inverness. The road runs along the side of Loch Ness, and is cut out of a very steep rocky declivity, in many places finely shaded with trees. From this station we had the most beautiful view of Loch Ness, and the best point in my opinion is from that narrow overhanging shelf called the Black Rock, about fifteen miles from Inverness. You command a view of the lake in its utmost extent from Fort Augustus to Dochfour. The lake is about twenty-three miles in length, uncommonly straight; the outline waves very little. It is confined by steep declivities on each side, which are covered with wood at their bases, particularly on the north side. It has the appearance of a narrow valley running from south-west to north-east. Towards Dochfour it appears to be separated by a green woody promontory; but the one division quickly terminates, and the other forms the broad rapid river Ness, which, like its parent lake, never freezes. The eastern extremity of Loch Ness, almost shaded in every point with green wavy woods, is uncommonly beautiful and picturesque, and gives a softness to this view of it which is not possessed by the view from the descent of Corryarrick upon Fort Augustus. The latter view is uncommonly wild, and very similar to some of the wildest lakes of the *rough bounds*, as there is little wood on the western extremity. From the eastern extremity of Loch Ness the road proceeds to Inverness through a finely wooded and cultivated country. The hills on the north have a very picturesque appearance, especially Tom-na-heurich, a small eminence covered with green wood which is so regular that it seems to have been formed by art. It was dark before we reached Inverness—whence I have the pleasure of addressing you—with the comfortable prospect before me of performing the rest of the journey with greater convenience,—I can scarcely hope with greater amusement. Adventures and hardships, however disagreeable for the present, are extremely pleasant to recollect, as they elevate a person in his own imagination and increase the idea of his own power. From Inverness we propose to take horses and proceed by Fortrose and Cromarty to Tain, and perhaps to Dunrobin. After retracing our steps to Tain we visit Dingwall, the mineral waters of Strathpeffer, and the vitrified fort of Knockfarrel—which is reckoned superior to Craig Phadrick—and proceed by Beauley and the Aird country to Urquhart and Glen Morrison, whence we return to Inverness. As there is little probability of our being wrecked in the Pentland Firth, as we mean to keep at a very respectable distance, you will hear some strictures upon Inverness, Ross, and perhaps Sutherland at my return. I am not so much delighted with the Inverness pronunciation as a certain female traveller of redoubted intrepidity, and am still more inclined to deny their pretensions to the classical English idiom; but perhaps Mrs Murray intended to compensate her injustice to the Hawick pronunciation by bepraising that of Inverness. The Borderers, you know, never admitted the Highland superiority in any respect; and I shall certainly dispute their pretensions to a correct English pronunciation.

To Dr R[obert] A[nderson].

NAIRN, *September* 11, 1800.

DEAR SIR,—Of every chapter in the book of Fate, the most disastrous, to my apprehension, is the chapter of Accidents. The great Johnson was accustomed to deny that a man's genius was dependent on wind and weather; but as a traveller he must undoubtedly have experienced that his temper, if not his genius, was dependent on every wind that blows. I had determined to begin this epistle with a violent satire upon the weather; but recollecting that this would demonstrate nothing but my own chagrin, I shall content myself with stating that a succession of misty days has not only induced us to renounce the journey to Ross, but occupied all the time we intended to devote to it, and that we are just arrived in Nairn, in such bad humour as to exult with a kind of malicious joy that the weather is still little better.

The first days of our stay in Inverness were occupied in traversing the town and its environs, where we beheld indeed very little that is not to be seen in every town. It contains some elegant buildings, but no regular streets or squares of neat houses. The two principal streets run nearly east and west, while that which contains the Town House and the most elegant buildings runs along their western ends from the bridge of the Ness towards the south. Many of the houses are of considerable antiquity, and have the arms of some Highland chieftain sculptured on a large slab inserted in the wall, from having been the town houses of these chieftains in feudal times. The quay might be considerably improved, though the shore is too flat and the water too shallow to admit of a good harbour being formed. But the finest view of Inverness is from the eminence above Muirtown as you ascend Craig Phadrick, one of the eminences of that ridge which conceals the Fraser country, or Aird. Here the apparent regularity of the arrangement and elegance of the structures greatly exceeds reality.

Craig Phadrick is now planted with wood, and all its sides are thickly overgrown with furze, which renders access extremely difficult. On the top are the remains of one of those singular ancient structures termed vitrified forts, which demonstrate the former existence of an art unknown to the moderns. On the south side, when you approach the top, you perceive distinctly the vestiges of a mound or exterior wall containing many vitrified masses. When you reach the summit a green level space presents itself, enclosed on every side with the remains of a rampart, forming a long square, rounded apparently at the angles, though this might be the effect of the ruin of the walls. The exterior rampart is of the same form, but approaches the interior wall more nearly at the long sides than at the small. As we ascended the hill we perceived a particular species of plum-pudding stone, consisting chiefly of small masses of feltspar and brown sand, consolidated and hard as granite. It seemed, therefore, extremely probable that the fire which was able to consolidate the loose nodules of a stone so infusible as feltspar, would certainly scorify and reduce to a state resembling pumice the softer stones which it might meet. Besides, I was somewhat sceptical on the subject of the vitrified forts, and therefore examined the remains with considerable attention at two different times. The first time, having only carried a hammer with me, my doubts were not removed; but afterwards, having procured a man with a mattock and shovel to dig, I was satisfied concerning the artificial vitrification of the walls. On both sides of the wall we found the masses which remain vitrified to a slag, while the middle or intermediate space was filled with large loose stones untouched by the fire, their interstices being jammed full of others of a smaller size. In many of the interstices of these stones we found a considerable quantity of charcoal powder. In the middle, too, of the plain space has been a well. It is now dry and filled up with earth, though its situation is very apparent.

Where the ridge of which Craig Phadrick forms a part terminates near the sea, enormous rent and shattered rocks of feltspar and plum-pudding stone emerge from the declivity.

Some persons have suggested that the vitrification was probably accidental in these forts; but from the most attentive observation I was induced to adopt the contrary opinion, especially as the regularity of it seems completely to preclude this idea.

The situation of the forts of Duncan, of Macbeth, and of Oliver Cromwell was pointed out to us, but hardly one stone remains upon another in any of them.

On the 5th I crossed the Beauley and went along the shore to Red Castle in quest of my Sanscrit friend Mr Hamilton. The country is fertile, but the soil is thin. Red Castle is an ancient pile fortified with turrets, but rather a strong house than a castle. Mr Grant, its present proprietor, has surrounded it with plantations. From this station there is a fine view of Aird, a country beautifully diversified with hill and dale, and at this time peculiarly picturesque from the great variety of shades produced by the ripe and ripening corn, the meadows and pasture-fields, and the trees of different colours. The day, however, was by no means favourable for a view.

On the 6th we dined with Provost Inglis, and conversed concerning the state of the town, Ossian's poems, and Highland antiquities, in which we found him by no means deficient in information. He told me that MacPherson had at first obtained many of his Gaelic poems from an uncle of his own, whom the Provost recollected, and who was a herbalist, and curious in ancient songs. He was told by Mr Home that MacPherson had made some progress in a translation of these poems in verse, when, accidentally showing them to the author of *Douglas*, he advised him to publish them in measured prose.

On the 7th, as the mist did not permit us to proceed to Ross as we intended, we rode to Rellich. But proceeding by mistake along the Glen Morrison road till we had reached the vicinity of Dochfour, we visited that beautiful scene. The mist was not so dense in the vale as on the mountains, but impeded our vision extremely. We beheld a scene of green sloping woods and trees of various shades of colour on both sides of the Ness which might have vied with the sweetest scenes of fairyland, but what resemblance it had to reality was more than we could determine.

From Dochfour we proceeded across the hills to Rellich, the seat of Mr Fraser, eight miles from Inverness and two from the Beauley river. The environs are well wooded, and there are several genteel houses in the immediate vicinity which we endeavoured to see during the two days we remained at Rellich, but the mist seldom permitted us to see farther than thirty yards. I walked up a small romantic glen, termed the Beg, through a considerable part of which Mr Fraser has drawn a winding path. The narrow scene permitted me to see its beauty in despite of the mist, but it is difficult to describe it in appropriate language. The beauty of such a scene must always consist in the different shades of the trees which cover the declivities, the intermixture of white rock and red earth. The glen is terminated by an abrupt white rock of considerable height, over which I was informed Mr Fraser intended to conduct a stream of water.

As the mist still continued, we were forced to return to Inverness, whence on the following day we proceeded to Culloden House. It is an elegant modern structure, surrounded with fine plantations. To the south-west of this lies the bleak heath where the fatal battle of 1746 was fought which decided the fate of the ancient Stuart line. Mr Fraser informed me that he had heard a Captain MacDonald of Breakish in Sky repeat *Temora.*

As we found it impossible now to see Ross in its beauty, we submitted with a very bad grace to the privation and took the road to Fort George, accompanied by Captains Clunes and Brown. Near Culloden we saw a fine Druidical circle, which we did not examine accurately. On the moor within a mile of Castle Stewart we found two, which we examined. One consisted of three concentric circles of large stones; the other consisted of two adjacent circles of smaller stones, which almost touched each other at the circumference. These are at a small distance from the larger circle. Castle Stewart is a fine ruin, but not older than the last century. There is nothing remarkable in the structure. We proceeded through Campbelton—a small town—to Fort George, situated on a promontory which runs far into the Moray Firth, the neck of which is so low that at a moderate distance the fort has the appearance of an island. The fort is of considerable strength, but seems to be commanded by the height over Campbelton. The works were in the form of an irregular square. Here we took leave of our military friends, and proceeded towards Nairn over the moor where Macbeth is said to have encountered the witches. Though we kept a sharp look-out for them we were not equally fortunate, and arrived safely at Nairn without being overwhelmed with chagrin. Indeed, so moderate were my expectations, that I should have been completely satisfied had they announced me a professorship in Aberdeen or St Andrews instead of the thaneship of Ross or Cawdor; but unfortunately I am still forced to subscribe myself your plain old friend.

To Dr R[obert] A[nderson].

ABERDEEN, *September* 19, 1800.

DEAR SIR,—After having traversed a considerable part of the east coast I do not find that we have any reason to regret the time occupied in surveying the more bold, wild, and romantic scenery of the west, in comparison of which the aspect of the east coast is insufferably flat and tame. The general appearance of the coast from Fort

George to Aberdeen is that of a flat declivity, diversified with low rising grounds. The surface is naturally a brown unvaried heath unbroken by rocks, but considerably altered by cultivation, which is much superior to that on the west coast, and has superinduced the green plain, the red fallow, and yellow corn-field. This district is intersected by various rivers of considerable size, which rush with rapidity from the passes of the mountain regions above the coast.

The small town of Nairn is more remarkable for being the chief of a small shire, and for the industry of its inhabitants, than for the regularity of its plan or the beauty of its situation. On our way to Forres we passed by Inchoch, Brodie, and Dalvey, seats which rather display the marks of antiquity than of elegance. We had likewise a distant view of the Castle of Darnaway, situated amid an extensive wood. We likewise saw Findhorn, a small town on the coast; and almost opposite to it the high grounds which lead to Cromarty. Fortrose, on the opposite side of the Moray Firth to Fort George, seems a most beautiful situation. The shore is skirted with high sand-hills. The approach to Forres is uncommonly beautiful and picturesque, the steeple towering above the houses, and surmounted on the right by a rising ground shaded with trees. Nearly half a mile from the town is the famous obelisk supposed to have been erected in memory of a convention with the Danes, an opinion corroborated by the appearance of two kings joining hands among the sculptured figures. The sculptured figures are for the most part in a state of high preservation; but the inscription resisted all my efforts to decipher, as it was hardly possible to distinguish the corrosions of the stone, by the weather, from the figures of the letters, which appeared to resemble considerably those of the Runic inscription at Bew Castle in Cumberland. The obelisk is above twenty feet in height, and somewhat shattered on the top, covered with sculptures and inscriptions on every side. Soon after we left Forres we saw at a little distance the ruins of Kinlossie Abbey, which we did not examine. They seemed to be of considerable extent, but greatly defaced. Between Forres and Elgin the road passes through a flat uninteresting district, but well cultivated, though the heath displays itself in every interval of cultivation. Elgin is a town of considerable size, and contains some good houses. It lies at the foot of a green eminence, on which a castle once stood which commanded the town.

The ruins of Elgin Cathedral are grand and impressive from their extent and the height and massiness of the walls and fragments. On the north, the front, and gateway with a finely sculptured Saxon arch, are almost entire, but the window over the gateway is shattered. The side walls are mostly demolished, but some elegantly finished arches of windows and doors still remain. The chapter-house, a fine cupola ornamented in the Gothic style and supported by a single pillar in the middle, is in a high state of preservation. The remains of the chancel, with the portico and gallery,—the pillars of which are almost entire,—are extremely venerable; but I regretted the destruction of the great east window between the rows, which must have had a very magnificent effect. The ruins of Elgin Abbey are much more august than any that I have seen, and excel equally in grandeur of the general effect and minuteness of the ornaments. We regretted that our time did not permit us to visit the magnificent remains of Pluscarden Abbey, five miles to the south-west of Elgin.

From Elgin we proceeded to Fochabers, over a district well wooded but discriminated by no characteristic scenery, and soon perceived the red, broken, and lofty banks of the Spey. The Spey descends with prodigious violence from the high inland district of Badenoch, but we did not see it in its magnificence. In its ordinary state it is not superior to the Tweed. The lower part of Strathspey is very fertile, and the greater part of the district is well sheltered with wood. The insipid bleak country by which it is surrounded causes it to be considered as beautiful. Fochabers is a neat country town, and Castle Gordon a magnificent pile surrounded with venerable woods. The scenery along the river seems to be extremely romantic towards Balrinnes, if I may judge from a distant glance.

From Fochabers the country becomes more bleak and heathy towards Keith, but the population and cultivation do not appear to decrease. Within two miles of Keith we saw another considerable village, termed New Mills. The brown heath is mottled over with green grazing grounds and fields of corn; the sides of the rivulets are green and lightly shaded with trees. Between Keith and Huntly, a small town similar to the former, we passed the braes of Balloch, a rising ground covered with low stunted heath lightly sprinkled with stones; and then, crossing the Deveron, a rapid river, reached Huntly. Unfortunately the Marquis of Huntly and a shooting-party had occupied the inn completely, and being unable to procure any tolerable apartments, we resolved to proceed to Leith Hall, the seat of Major-General Hay. The night was extremely dark, our horses were very tired, and we soon discovered that the driver was but little acquainted with the road. We were too much fatigued to relish an adventure, and rather inclined to sleep than to meditate on our situation, which we perceived was dangerous enough, though we could not make it better. We entered Strathbogie, and after having repeatedly stuck fast in the mud, we at last got out of the chaise and resolved to walk till the roads became better. After we had proceeded about two miles we found ourselves puzzled how to go forward. We listened, but no chaise could be heard approaching; we hallooed, but could hear no answer. We returned upon our steps, and when we had walked about a mile and a half we met the driver advancing with our portmanteaus tied upon one horse, having left the other, who objected to proceeding farther, with the chaise. When we had gone a mile we discovered that something had been forgot in the chaise, and I was obliged to return for it. By these manœuvres we continued to occupy about five hours, and reached Leith Hall at two o'clock in the morning, when we learned with horror that the whole family were absent; and the servant, who took us, as we were informed, for *vagabonds,* refused all admission. After various explanations we got admission, and waited till the family arrived.

Leith Hall is situated in the Garioch, and is an old square tower modernised by the addition of two wings united by a gateway. It is nearly two miles distant from Gordon Hall, and is covered by a fir plantation on the heathy hill by which it is surmounted, where there is a marble quarry. On the 15th we went to the hill of Noth,—the highest in the neighbourhood,—on the top of which is a vitrified fort, of considerably greater extent than that of Craig Phadrick, though of similar form. It is a large oblong square of about 1000 feet in circumference. The wall is about twelve feet in height at present above the level of the green plain which contains the pit or well, which is still filled with water. The wall has been above twelve feet thick at the base, and, if I may judge by its ruins, above twenty feet high. It is only vitrified on the out and in side, but the heat seems seldom to have reached the middle of the wall. Some of the shepherds had dug away in one place about half the wall from the interior, and gave us an opportunity of seeing the inside, which was not vitrified but formed of loose stones, like the central part of the wall of Craig Phadrick. We were afterwards informed by Dr Skene of Aberdeen that he found in the interstices of the mound, sticking between two fused stones, a piece of half-consumed wood. We saw a considerable quantity of charcoal. There is some basalt to be found on the declivity of the hill, and most of the stones are strongly magnetic. We observed indubitable traces of an exterior wall which surrounded the upper part of the hill.

The view from Noth is wild and desolate rather than picturesque. The nearest districts are covered with a brown uninterrupted heath, variegated with meadows and corn-fields, with few trees except in the immediate vicinity of *great houses*. It is bordered on the south side by the Dee's mountains, and northwards expands as far as the

Paps of Caithness. The long hill of Benachie is one of the most picturesque objects, and there is a beautiful view of Huntly, in the vale of Strathbogie, towards the south-east.

On the 16th we went to view the ruins of Kildrummie, about thirteen miles from Leith Hall. About two miles to the south of Leith Hall I saw the ruin of Drumennir Tower, which the proprietor had demolished. The wall is about nine feet thick, and the cement is exceedingly strong. It consists of a square united to a half square, which contains the staircase. About a mile beyond Drumennir is the manse of Rhynie, a very beautiful scene. Two miles farther I reached Craig, and traversed a wild romantic glen denominated the Den of Craig. It has been a barren uninteresting hollow, but the father of the present proprietor exhibited much taste in humouring nature. His sister, Miss A. Gordon, conducted me through the windings of the labyrinth, and pointed out the various beauties of the scene. One side of the rivulet is planted with firs, and the other with oak, mountain-ash, birch, &c. The various shades of the trees, the windings and projections of the banks, and the different falls of water,—which are more picturesque from the surrounding scenery than from their own height,—form a spot equally beautiful and romantic. The Castle of Craig consists of a winged square tower, or a square and a half like that of Drumennir, and the new house is connected with the castle. In the ballad of *Edom o' Gordon*, repeated in this country, there is a verse which is in none of the printed editions. The subject of that ballad is said to be the taking of the Castle of Corgarff by a notorious robber of the Gordon family.

In the answer of the lady to the expostulation of her daughter is the following verse,—

"O, I wad yield to Craig or Gicht,
　　Or ony wordy man;
But I winna yield to that rank riever,
　　Edom the fell Gordonne."

On the hills above Craig there is a considerable quantity of asbestus found, much consolidated. The hill termed the Buck of the Cabroth is about 600 feet higher than Noth, which is 1800 feet above the level of the sea. The Cabroth is a sequestered mountain-district. The declivities of the surrounding hills are heathy, but the vale is well cultivated. In the severe months of winter it is impossible to penetrate into this district.

The flat of Kildrummie is a heathy wild, which looks the wilder from the contrast of its cultivated spots. The Castle of Kildrummie appears to have been of considerable size; but the greater part of the ruins have been demolished, by the consent of the proprietor, to build farmhouses. On three sides it presents a front flanked with strong large round towers. The side of the great gate has been semicircular, and probably surmounted with another tower over the gateway. The fort is supposed to be about 800 years old, and was the place where Robert Bruce placed his queen under the charge of his brother Nigel, who was executed for treason by Edward I. when Kildrummie was taken by the English. The view from an eminence above Kildrummie is exceedingly wild, but it is extremely difficult to analyse it. It is not picturesque. It appears to be a desert, though intersected by numerous cornfields, and containing many villages, cottages, and elegant houses. The heath, the natural covering of the country, is dun—short and uniform—uninterrupted by rocks or precipices. The Don escapes through a steep chasm of the surrounding mountains, the one side of which is abrupt and rocky. The other is lightly shaded with green firs, adjacent to which rises a brown heathy eminence, smooth and conical.

Ascending the hills above Kildrummie, the beautiful strath of the Don expands before the eye, variegated with green and yellow corn-fields, intermixed with long strips of heath, as the natural character of the country seems to be similar to that of the Garioch and Strathbogie. The Don is skirted on both sides by numerous plantations, none of them very ancient. Towards the right it appears still more beautiful. Towards the south the view extends over numerous ridges of uniform heath, which tower above each other and appear through partial depressions of the nearest. Returning in the evening from Craig, it was almost impossible to trace the path in the dark. I succeeded, however, tolerably well till I reached the Bogie, in attempting to cross which, over large stones, I stumbled, and was almost drowned in the river.

On the 17th I walked to Dunedeir, a small green hill about five miles to the north-east of Leith Hall, where there is the side wall of a castle with a large window, which is an exceeding fine vista at a distance. On this hill I found likewise the remains of a vitrified fort, about the same size with that of Craig Phadrick. The vitrification here is more perfect and less encumbered with rubbish than that on Noth, as the loose stones have probably been removed to build the castle upon the same site. On the west side there is a rude arch about three feet high, which probably served for entrance to the fort. All the stones and rocks on this hill and its vicinity exhibit marks of fire, and are magnetic. They are chiefly of granite. The view from Dunedeir is rather extensive than various. It commands a view of the Garioch, a flat fertile district when compared with the rest of the east coast we have passed. The horizon is skirted with brown, unbroken, heathy hills. The principal objects are Benachie, a long hill which rises to a considerable height about the middle of the ridge, where, we were informed, there is a fortress, whether vitrified or not we could not learn; and Christ's Kirk [on the Green], the scene of a ludicrous poem in the fifteenth century, and until lately that of the Sleepy Fair, a kind of wake celebrated between sunset and sunrising. On the 18th I traced the windings of the Bogie to Huntly, the

Strath being neither beautiful nor picturesque; but it is better, being extremely fertile, and forming a fine contrast to the barren heathy mountains by which it is bounded on every side.

On the 19th we left Leith Hall early in the morning, and proceeded over part of the Garioch by the foot of Benachie to Inverury, a small straggling town, or rather village, only remarkable for the victory which Robert Bruce gained here. The country continues flat, fertile, and uninteresting. In this vicinity, too, was fought the battle of Harlaw in 1411, where the MacDonalds experienced a check from which they never recovered. From the Don the country is more and more sheltered with wood to the environs of Aberdeen, the elegant seats are more numerous, and the population considerably greater. The approach to Aberdeen is extremely beautiful after the sea appears in sight;

and in our situation its beauty was enhanced by the flat insipid country we had left. Only a' small part of the old town first presents itself, and no more is seen till the whole bursts upon the eye, when we beheld a long line of houses extending parallel to the shore, with various steeples and towers of different forms elevated far above the rest, and exhibiting a very fine appearance. Next we saw the new town, of considerable extent and population, though not much distinguished for regularity or elegance. We have walked over a considerable part of the town and visited the quay, which is of considerable extent. The new quay is but lately finished at a vast expence. The harbour seems to be shallow, but safe: it extends about a mile inland. To-morrow we visit the colleges and professors, and afterwards we enter upon a more romantic part of the east coast than we have hitherto traversed. The town dialect of Aberdeen seems not, to my ear, inferior to that of Inverness. You will probably, however, question the taste of a Borderer in pronunciation.

To Dr R[obert] A[nderson].

Dunkeld, *September* 24, 1800.

Dear Sir,—You are about to find me much better satisfied with the east coast than in my last. The character of the scenery in the district we have traversed since leaving Aberdeen is entirely different from that between Aberdeen and Inverness. It rejects [comparison] in blank insipid aspect, and vies with that of the west, if not in majestic and savage grandeur, yet in the wildly romantic and picturesque.

In my strictures on the town of Aberdeen I forgot to mention a cross of some antiquity, ornamented with curious bas-reliefs of some of the Scotish princes, and in particular with one of Queen Mary. The two colleges are not remarkable for structure or architecture. I waited on Professors Gerard and Jack of King's College, and Principal Brown and Professors Glennie and Kidd of Marischal College, by means of whom I was shown everything curious in the colleges and libraries. In neither of the libraries are there any printed catalogues. I enquired without effect in both libraries for *The General and Special Physicks*, systematised by Wm. Black in 1697 for both colleges; *Logic and General Metaphysics*, by the two Colleges of St Andrews; *Pneumatics and Special Metaphysics*, by Edinburgh College; *General and Special Ethics*, by the College of Glasgow. If any of these papers subsist in the archives of the college, they are unknown to the professors.

My bibliographic enquiries concerning Scotish antiquities—*Complaynt of Scotland, Godly Sangs, Lady Scotland's Lamentation*, Bellenden's *Virgil*, Lindsay's *Satires* (1603-44), *Black Acts* (James V. to Charles I.), Cardinal Beaton's *Catechism* (1540), Bishop Hamilton's *Catechism* (woodcuts), Forbes's *Cantus* (1st edition), *Don, a Poem* (about 1654), &c.—terminated in discovering that there is a portrait in Forbes's *Funerals*, 4to, 1635. How mortifying!

I saw a curious MS. History of Scotland (Weemio quodam), in which there are many curious remarks concerning the Gaelic language, &c. Unfortunately the author begins at Japhet. Also Lindsay of Pitscottie's *History of Scotland from James II. to James VI.*, " transcribed from an ancient copy for the use of the King's College of Aberdeen by Mr J. Hunter, sometyme student there, May 15, 1729."

There are likewise several volumes of Juridical Papers, Acts of Assembly, &c.; a fine MS. of Ovid; the *Shaster*, written on palm-leaf; and some Persian Poems presented to King's College by Sir John MacPherson.

In Marischal College there is a small but curious museum. Their MSS. are more numerous, but chiefly religious, some of them very finely written. An elegant Hebrew Bible, collated by Kennicott; a fine MS. of Martial; a fine MS. of some parts of Cicero; a translation of Aristotle's *Poetics* by L. Aretino. Mr Glennie informed me that Dr Beattie did not know the author of the poem *Albania*,* and had lost his copy of the poem.

* Leyden afterwards republished this poem, along with Wilson's *Clyde*, &c., under the title of *Scotish Descriptive Poems; with some Illustrations of Scotish Literary Antiquities.* 12mo. Edin., 1803.

On the 21st we left Aberdeen to ascend the Dee, a large and beautiful river. The day was unpropitious in the highest degree when we set out, but soon became clear. As we ascended the river the scenery became continually more interesting. The banks are green, sheltered with wood, and elegant houses are frequent for the first ten miles. The view is continually bounded by bleak heathy mountains scattered over with gray stones, and but little broken by rocks or precipices. Invercainy is a soft woody scene, but a very wild heathy moor interposes between it and Kincardine O'Neil. At Kincardine O'Neil the scenery becomes truly picturesque and romantic, though it hardly aspires at the grand or sublime. The view is not extensive, but the groups are minute, and unite numerous beauties in a small compass. The windings of the Dee, with its steep red banks fringed with wood; the cornfields and meadows on the haughs; the plantations climbing the declivities; and the black heathy tops of the hills, intermingled with gray rocks, formed a scene at once various, picturesque, and beautiful,—a scene which varied its aspect with every winding of the river. Kincardine is but a small village, though the largest on the Dee. Between Kincardine and the pass of Ballater the character of the scenery continues the same, and its variety defies description. The pass of Ballater is a deep chasm in a range of red granite which runs across the bed of the Dee, and threatens to intercept all intercourse with the superior district of Braemar from the coast. Its declivity is exceedingly bold, and, like its base, covered with wood. Before we reached this pass we saw at a distance the mineral springs of Pannanich, near a hunting-seat of * termed Dee Castle.

We followed the windings of the Dee into Braemar, where the scenery becomes more bold and grand, though it remains equally romantic. Lofty ridges and spires of dun hills, steep declivities, narrow passes, and overhanging rocks present themselves more frequently, while the trees—especially the firs—become more huge and tall. In this elevated district the Dee still continues a considerable and rapid river, tracing its course very ingeniously, where no person could tell beforehand from viewing the ground whether it will be found to run up or down. At last we reached Braemar Castle, surrounded with a wall and moat, of great height, forming an irregular square, with small round turrets on the sides. Its situation is extremely romantic, on

* Name omitted in MS.

the banks of the Dee, between two high heathy ridges. The vale widens at Castletown of Braemar, where there is a cluster of cottages. The Gaelic of Braemar is deemed extremely barbarous. From Castletown we walked up the Dee to Mar Lodge, a hunting-seat situated in a beautiful glen near the sources of the Dee, which is almost shrouded with wood as well as the surrounding mountains. We saw a fine cataract within a mile of Mar Lodge, but had no time to proceed to the Linn of Dee, which, we were informed, is more remarkable for the narrow chasm than for the height of the waterfall.

From Braemar we proceeded up Glen Beg, a bleak dismal unfertile valley, to the pass of * , which resembles considerably the pass of Corryarrick, as the declivities where the road

* Name omitted in MS.

runs are green, plashy, and mossy, with numerous loose stones scattered over them. The mountains which confine the pass are bleak, lofty, and sterile, gray and rocky near their summits. We soon began to descend into Glenshee, where the ground is cultivated enough to display the poverty of the soil. This is, however, to be expected in such an elevated district. At the Spittal of Glenshee (spittal signifies village) the glen falls into a wide, fertile, and romantic strath, which, however, still retains the name of Glenshee. After emerging from Mar Forest the country seems extremely naked, though occasionally sprinkled with trees and plantations. The view of the entrance of the pass from the spittal is wild and grand. The elevation of the hills is extremely bold, and their declivities, though steep, are green almost to the top. The hill which shuts up the pass on the north is steep and heathy where it fronts the pass, but green and rocky towards the spittal or village. The road then passes through a high but fertile country, which, though not so interesting as the mountain scenery in Mar Forest, has an air of grandeur from the elevation of the mountains, which rise above each other in rude and shaggy magnificence. The large river Shee passes through the valley, receiving in its course numerous streams, which descend through woody picturesque glens. After ascending a bleak heath, a scene entirely different expanded before us. The wide level district of Strathmore, with its towns and villages stretching far to the east and west, impresses with vivid pleasure the traveller emerging from the passes of the Grampians, where the scanty horizon is bounded by bleak heathy hills deformed by gray rocks. We now descended rapidly upon Marly, in the parish of Kinloch, a village sheltered with wood, which lies upon Loch Drumelzie, a fine sheet of water, but too naked to be picturesque. As the sun descended we had a peep of the small Loch of Clunie. From Marly we proceeded along the Dunkeld road, part of which runs along a bleak barren moor, but commands a fine view of a chain of lakes which extend from the foot of the Stormont Hills almost to Dunkeld. The names of the lochs which compose this chain are Loch Stormont, the Black Loch, the White Loch, Loch Finess, Loch Ree, Loch Dramalie, Loch Clunie, Loch Butterston, Loch of the Lows. Loch Clunie is not equal to Loch Dramalie as a sheet of water, neither are its shores picturesque or striking, as they are extremely naked. It contains, however, a small island, with an old stronghouse shaded by tall trees, where the Admirable Crichton is said to have been born. Loch Butterston and the Loch of the Lows are more picturesque than any of the others, and resemble the Cumberland lakes in softness. The last is surmounted by the high shaggy rocks which impend over Dunkeld, wooded like the Trosachs, and extremely romantic. Dunkeld is a small irregular town, the most remarkable object in which is its cathedral, of no great antiquity. It is a stately edifice; but part is a ruin and part is refitted for the parochial church, like the abbey of Melrose. The high heathy hills by which the town is surrounded are covered to the top with plantations, which render the scene uncommonly beautiful. On the north side of the town the White Crag, a precipice of considerable elevation, rises over the shaggy declivities beneath it with a formidable air, and is hardly inferior to the Cumbrian Wallow. The woods around Atholl House and gardens are distinguished by the great size and height of the trees. We went to visit the Hermitage, termed Ossian's Hall, and crossed the majestic Tay. We entered the woods on the opposite side of the Tay and ascended the impetuous Braan, which was swollen by rain, and thundered over a bed of large loose stones. Ossian's Hall is a very elegant modern summer-house; but I see no propriety in the appellation, except that the drawing door by which you enter is ornamented with a foppish picture of the ancient bard. We saw the fall in great perfection, but the height is not great. The mirror on the roof produces a fine effect by representing the water of the cataract as ascending with prodigious force and velocity as if from an immense caldron. We ascended the Braan to the Rumbling Linn, a waterfall the appearance of which was very tremendous, though the fall was hardly equal to that of the Hermitage. The stream passes with dreadful velocity through a narrow oblique chasm, which is almost dammed up by the fall of an immense rock. The evening had darkened around us before our return. To-morrow we proceed for Blair Atholl and Loch Tay, from which we propose to return by Dunkeld to Perth. Though one seems to breathe a little more freely in the champaign country after being so long pent up in the narrow glens of Braemar, yet I greatly doubt that the Lothians will appear uninteresting and insipid after this tour. Yet after all the scenes of the Highlands, the banks of the Tweed and the Teviot still make a very respectable figure in my recollection.

To Dr R[obert] A[nderson].

PERTH, *September* 30, 1800.

DEAR SIR,—I may now congratulate myself on a safe escape from the Indians of Scotland, as our friend Ramsay denominates the Highlanders, and have no reason to regret our neglecting his advice with respect to the Norwegian voyage, which he strongly recommended instead of the northern tour. The districts of Atholl and Breadalbane are not inferior in picturesque beauty or sublimity to the scenes we visited in the West Highlands. Having procured horses at Dunkeld, we ascended the Tay for eight miles. The view is somewhat confined. The strath is well cultivated, and the tops of the lofty hills by which it is bounded covered with heath. From Logierait we ascended the Tummel—a large majestic river of greater impetuosity than the Tay—to its conflux with the Garrie. The situations of Dalguise and Kinnaird below Logierait are extremely beautiful. From the junction of the Tummel and Tay the scenery becomes still more interesting and romantic till you reach the environs of Fascalie, which may almost vie with the inimitable Trosachs in variety of picturesque beauty. The declivity is excessively irregular, and various eminences rise to a considerable height from the valley, shaded with wood of different tints, surmounted with lofty ridges of rocks and scaurs of reddish earth. This beautiful situation lies just at the entrance of the narrow rugged defile of Killicrankie. Before entering the Pass of Killicrankie I passed through some fine plantations to see the fall of the Tummel. Its height is nearly the same as that of the Rumbling Bridge, but the body of water is considerably greater. The Tummel is here a rough impetuous stream, not so large as the Garrie, which runs here more deeply and smoothly than in almost any other part of its course. Killicrankie is a very narrow rugged defile. The declivities on both sides of the Garrie are covered with wood, and the whole scene is wild and romantic. Emerging from the pass, we entered the haughs where the battle was fought in which Dundee was victorious over a superior army. An obelisk near the roadside, which marks the place where the second in command fell, is generally mistaken for the spot where the general was slain. Dundee himself fell near Urrard House, at a stream termed Uisge na callec (*fons virginis*). The legend adds that it was prophesied he should fall when his horse drank of the stream of that name. Blair Atholl now appeared in view, surrounded with woods and plantations; but after the scene which we had left behind us it appeared neither very romantic nor interesting. We passed along the declivity descending from Lude, a fine seat which commands a view of Atholl valley, and soon after our arrival proceeded to visit the castle and grounds. Atholl Castle consists of two square towers united, or a long square with wings or projections near each end. The one tower was built by the Cummings, the other by the Stewarts, but in 1747 one half of its height was demolished. Probably the Duke of Atholl during the rebellion found reason to prefer a snug mansion for entertaining his friends and living comfortably, to a fort and garrison. The woods of Atholl are remarkable for the size of the trees, though not equal to those at Dunkeld. We went up the Tilt, a small but impetuous river, to that chain of small cascades generally denominated the York Cascade. They are five in number, and not very remarkable. Winding down the river a little we saw one natural and one artificial cascade both higher than any of the chain (Frederick Cascade). On the Tilt we saw the rock from which criminals were formerly thrown into the river, and on the opposite side the projecting ends of stone coffins, containing bones of great size. From Blair Atholl we rode about four miles to the falls of the Bruar. The bed of the river is a steep, jagged, irregular chasm torn in the solid limestone rock by the violence of the waters. Though the rains had not much retarded our journey, they had been considerable enough to swell the mountain torrents, and we beheld the Bruar rushing and foaming along with rage and violence. Its bed is so abrupt, and so little marked out by green banks and trees, that at a short distance we could only distinguish it by the sound. The banks, or rather precipices, of the Bruar are extremely naked, but are of late planted.* The Duke of Atholl has conducted a gravel walk on both sides of the river where the falls are most remarkable, and thrown two arches over it. The first fall is immediately beneath the lowest bridge, and is remarkable for dashing through a natural arch of the rock. A hut of twisted birch at the end of this bridge commands a fine view of the first chain of falls, which are none of them very high; but the succession is quick and the violence of the water great. The second chain of falls is superior to the first, particularly the lowest in the series, which is of considerable height. A neat birchen hut likewise commands a view of this chain.

* See Note F, p. 284.

The walk terminates with the view of a single fall which is not remarkable, above which the river becomes less wild and interesting.

We waited upon Mr MacLaggan, the minister of Blair Atholl, and had much conversation with him upon Highland antiquities and Ossian's poems. He is extremely zealous, and a man of great information.

He mentioned having seen in Lewis a round tower built without cement, the inside of which formed an inverted cone. The wall was double, and by his description it must have resembled the towers in Glenelg (Dalearlaway).

He showed me a great number of Gaelic poems in MS., both ancient and modern. He pointed out many poems and fragments published by MacPherson and Smith, and some that have never been translated, as *Conn Mac an Deirg mhie Drein*, but regretted having lost in America a completer copy of this poem. I recollect *Dan an Deirg, Dearg MacDeirg, The Death of Oscar, The Death of Gaul, The Sons of Usnoth, The Address to the Sun, Magnus, The Courtship of Ossian, The Hazard of the Fingalians,* or *Erragen of Sora.* He showed me three letters of MacPherson's, dated in 1760 and 1761, requesting his assistance, especially as he had heard that Mr MacLaggan's collections were more correct than common recitals. In these, Mr MacPherson mentions that he had traversed most of the Isles and North Highlands, and meditated an excursion to Mull, Lorn, and Perthshire. Mr MacLaggan told me that he gave him about thirteen poems; and in one of these letters MacPherson acknowledges the receipt of some poems from him, and makes some critical observations on them. He mentions that he had procured various MSS., and requests Mr MacLaggan to keep his eye on any that might fall in his way. He mentions also having found in one of these a poem of the epic kind, consisting of about 8000 lines, and says that he thinks it not inferior to the epics of other nations. He says that when MSS. fell in his way he always endeavoured to secure the poetical parts of them.

Mr MacLaggan told me that he had heard many of the poems of Ossian before MacPherson was born, and that he had made many collections of them when at school and college; that the recitals were not equally perfect, but that it was easy to distinguish the ancient style. Some of the MSS. he showed me were in the handwriting of the Rev. Mr MacArthur of Kilmore in Mull, whose father could never read or write the English language or character, though he corresponded constantly with his son in the Irish character while he studied at St Andrews. This he mentioned as a proof of the current use of the Irish character among the Highlanders, which he asserts was very common. He mentioned various songs concerning the MacGregors, and related that an infant who was taken in one of their predatory incursions, and adopted into the clan afterwards when they were proscribed, composed seventeen songs in their praise, and, among the rest, *MacGregor a Ruaro*.

We took leave of the venerable Mr MacLaggan, crossed the Garrie, and proceeded over a bleak heathy moor, till at the verge of a steep descent, covered with loose gray stones and young birches, Loch Tummel expanded before us, the beauty and softness of which is much increased by the striking contrast of the heathy and rugged hills by which it is surrounded. The borders of the lake are soft, green, and pastoral. The banks of the Tummel are beautiful and well wooded. There are few remains of Loch Tummel Castle, situated in a kind of island at the head of the lake, where Bruce in his greatest misfortunes was received by Duncan, son of Angus, Lord of the Isles. On the south-west Sheehallion, a lofty insulated mountain, towers in naked majesty.

After crossing another barren moor of considerable extent we approached the head of Strath-Tay, saw the ruin of Castle Garth, and a chain of waterfalls equal, if not superior, to the lowest of the Bruar. The heathy hills over Taymouth are covered with wood to their summits, which gives an air of softness and pastoral beauty to the country. Taymouth is embosomed in woods, through which avenues are conducted to some fine views of Loch Tay. The village of Kenmore is situated at the foot of the lake, of which it commands a very fine view. The north side of the loch near Kenmore is abrupt, shaggy, and covered with wood to the top of a high heathy hill. On the south side it is soft and picturesque,—yellow corn-fields, strips of trees, and green fields descending down the declivities to the verge of the lake. We went up the north side of Loch Tay to Killin, and returned on the south side. It is difficult to determine which side of it is most beautiful and sweetly picturesque. I prefer the view from the south side, as the range of hills is highest on the opposite side, where we saw the huge Ben Lawers with his top crowned with snow, beneath which extended a strip of heath, then a green field, then a field of yellow corn, with numerous copses of trees fringing the border of the lake. The head of Loch Tay is somewhat more wild, but continues extremely beautiful and picturesque to Killin and Kinnell, between the Lochy and Dochart, both large rapid rivers. At Kinnell is a small Druidical circle, which we did not see. About eight miles from Killin, on the south side of the lake, we saw the fall of the Dovecraig, which is extremely beautiful, and, next to the Fall of Fyres, the highest we had seen. Within two miles of Kenmore we saw the Fall of Acharn, which is as high, or perhaps higher, than the fall of the Dovecraig, but the descent is not so perpendicular. In order to reach this fall we entered a dark passage, by which we were conducted to a hermitage which fronts it. The view is exceedingly sublime and romantic, as the declivities are overgrown with wood. We descended the lake to Kenmore, and proceeding about two miles farther, saw the Druidical circle of Taymouth, which has originally consisted of three concentric circles of large stones, some of which are about eight and ten feet high; but as it stands in a fine corn-field, the exterior circle is a good deal destroyed by the farmer blowing up the huge unwieldy masses of which it is composed by gunpowder. We proceeded through the straggling village of Aberfeldie, which has a fine situation on the Tay, to Weem, situated beneath a steep overhanging bank, the declivity of which is covered by wood. We returned next morning to Moness, above Aberfeldie, to view the falls—which consist of two chains—the finest of which is the uppermost. The upper fall in this chain is little inferior to that of Taymouth Hermitage, which it likewise resembles in the close and hanging thickets which cover the declivities. The House of Moness, situated below the falls, is only distinguished by its situation, which is soft and romantic. We descended Strath Tay on the north side of the river, the banks of which are well wooded and cultivated, but do not appear to be romantic after Loch Tay and Taymouth. Near Logierait we crossed the bleak heathy hills between the Tummel and Tay, which are seldom traversed except by the shepherd and the sportsman. From the top of the ridge we had a very fine view of Fascalie and Bishoprick—as the strath is termed from having formerly been Church land—from the opposite side. At this elevation the scenery did not appear to such advantage as in our ride to Blair Atholl, but we were able to discriminate much better the relative situation of the objects we had formerly viewed more nearly. We descended to Logierait, a small irregular village, which was formerly the residence of the Breadalbane family. Here we crossed the ferry of the Tummel and proceeded to Dunkeld. On the 29th we left Dunkeld, and crossed the Tay on our way towards Perth. The day was exceedingly misty when we set out, but soon became clear, and permitted us to have a tolerable view of the country adjacent to the road. The banks of the Tay between Dunkeld and Perth are rather beautiful than romantic or picturesque. They are covered with wood and plantations, from the midst of which numerous elegant mansions emerge. The ground is fertile and highly cultivated. The character of the scenery is soft and sweet; but it pleases chiefly by displaying the combinations and effects of art, in a country possessing many natural beauties. The situation of the venerable Gothic pile of Murthly, on the south bank of the Tay, covered with woods towards the land, is extremely beautiful. Delvin, on the north side, is almost concealed by wood; but Stenton is a picturesque spot of wood and clustered white rocks. We passed beneath Birnam to Stanley, a small town the situation of which is extremely sweet and romantic, and proceeded to Taymount to see the Linn of Campsie, a small fall of the Tay, produced by three small islands, or rather rocks, crossing its channel and obstructing its passage. The winding banks of the Tay, steep and shaggy, with bushes immediately beneath the fall, are in my opinion more worthy of attention than the fall itself. We saw at a distance the ruin of Kinclaven Castle and the ancient pile of Stubhall, the situation of which is very romantic, and the ancient appearance of the castle harmonises with the corresponding scenery. The road to Scone presents various delightful views of the Tay and its soft cultivated banks, all of them characterised by simple elegance. Scone is a neat village, undistinguished by situation or scenery. Its only claim to attention is the venerable palace, so long the residence of the kings of Scotland. The form of the palace is a long square with two wings. It is extremely low, consisting of one sunk flat containing rooms for servants, one suite of apartments, and above these a range of garrets. Here are preserved several pieces of old furniture belonging to the royal family of Scotland, and, in particular, the hangings of a bed which were wrought by Queen Mary while confined in Lochleven Castle. There are several pictures, in particular two good ones of James V. and Mary of Guise. The ancient gallery where the Parliament of Scotland formerly met is very curious. From the window of the hall of state there is a fine view of the river Tay. We then crossed the moor of Scone, through some fine plantations, to St Martins, where we saw Mr MacDonald, &c. St Martins is situated low and covered by plantations, but has a very fine view of Dunsinan Hill, where Birnam Wood seems to have taken root. On the top there must be a vitrified fort. I saw some specimens of the vitrified stones at St Martins, as well as some fine agates and crystals from the top of the hill.

Mr MacDonald mentioned a singular fact with respect to Ossian. About thirty years ago, when at Airds in Appin, he heard a very old man repeat *Temora* till he was weary with listening. During the time of the repetition he compared it with MacPherson's translations, which appeared to him very much inferior to the original, the style of which was decidedly ancient.

From St Martins we proceeded to Perth along the Aberdeen road. The view of Perth as we descended upon the town is extremely beautiful. The declivities were covered with corn-fields and trees, and the green hills which surmount it on the north and south, especially that of Moncrieff, are soft and romantic, displaying many elegant mansions in their recesses. As you approach, the buildings are extremely good, and the plan of the town is very regular. Tay bridge is a noble object, and the views up and down the river are sweet and picturesque. The ruin of Castle Gowrie is in no respect remarkable, except from having been the scene of one of those obscure facts in history which afford a wide range for conjecture, but defy elucidation. Mr Morison has projected a work which combines the advantages of the pen and pencil in description, which is to be published in four numbers, each containing four plates. This series is to be accompanied with a description of the course of the river from the head of Loch Tay to the ocean, so that it is probable this delightful country will soon be better described than by the cursory sketches of any transient traveller like your humble servant, who am here to-day and away to-morrow.

To Dr T[homas] B[rown].

KINROSS, *October* 1, 1800.

DEAR SIR,— The most necessary qualities for a traveller are courage and patience. Perhaps your logic may reduce them to the same general quality, denominating the one active courage and the other passive. I fortified myself with numerous maxims concerning the efficacy of patience at the commencement of our tour, because I had frequently heard as well as learned by experience that a traveller is the very creature of chance, and peculiarly exposed to suffer disappointments. This stock served me tolerably well till I arrived in Perth and found that fate had another in store which had been entirely omitted in my calculations. The time which we spent in Aberdeenshire was so great, that we have found it impracticable to traverse Fife and see you in St Andrews. I therefore left Perth yesterday afternoon in that pleasant and amusing state of mind which is something between regret and chagrin, and does not appear to have been accurately described by philosophers. Whether it was the motion of the post-chaise, which gives a cheerful circulation to the fluids; whether it was the succession of new scenes or the succession of my own thoughts, I shall not pretend to determine; but I found by the time that we had gained the summit of Moncrieff

S

Hill I had regained my usual serenity. Here we paused to enjoy the view, which is delightful; and here it was that the Romans, advancing against our invincible ancestors, paused in astonishment, and, beholding the majestic Tay, imagined that they had discovered another Tiber. The range of the Grampian mountains bounds the horizon towards the north, and the fertile vale of Strathmore occupies the intermediate space, through which you trace the course of the Tay till your eye is arrested by the town of Perth, its spires and majestic bridge. The Kinnoul Crags, emerging boldly towards the river through the woods which skirt their bases and surround the romantic Kinfauns, are extremely grand and picturesque. Towards the east expand the rich and fertile Carse of Gowrie and the Firth of Tay. The view towards the south extends over the fertile and cultivated district of Strathearn, which has not the variety of the Strath of Tay, though it resembles it in softness and beauty. The Earn is a majestic river, but its banks are low, and here not well sheltered with wood. Following its windings, the eye passes over Abernethy and rests upon the green range of the Lomond Hills. After passing the Brig of Earn, we left the Highlands behind us with regret and ascended the range of the Ochil Hills, from which we had another fine view of Strathearn. The scene now became bleak and uninteresting, till we perceived the surface of Loch Leven glimmering like silver in the retiring beams of the sun. The lake, a wide and beautiful bason, spreads in the bosom of a low range of hills. Its sides are green, but flat and uninteresting, from the declivities being almost void of wood, as well as their slope extremely small. After the many accounts of the beauty of the lake, which every person repeats, I confess it by no means answered my expectation. The chief defect, however, lies in the insipidity of the surrounding scenery. The island, with its ruin, has a very fine effect; and if the environs were not so bleak the sheet of water might be deemed very beautiful. Kinross House, an old Gothic structure, is quite embowered by an ancient copse. The town of Kinross presents to the traveller no particular object of attention: one country town is commonly like another when the manners of the people are not strikingly different. But I do not recollect that these objects of which I am attempting to give you such a minute description—— No matter, you have at least an opportunity of comparing your own recollections with those of another, and consequently in indulging in a trifling degree that singular propensity of our nature to attend to the feelings of another in a situation which we have experienced; and while you philosophise, be pleased to recollect that I have the pleasure of being yours very sincerely,

JOHN LEYDEN.

NOTES.

NOTE A, p. 13.

The Water-Horse (*Each Uisge*).

"The superstitious opinions of the ancient Highlanders seem to have borrowed their tone, in a great measure, from the nature of the country which they inhabited. Living, as they did, amongst dreary wastes, and rugged mountains; their progress from one place to another impeded, frequently, by the rapid torrent, or wide stretched lake; often, in their journeys, sinking under the pressure of fatigue and hunger, or borne down by the rigors of an inclement sky,—their imagination was naturally led to ascribe every disaster to the influence of superior powers, in whose character the predominating feature necessarily was malignity towards the human race.

"Every lake had its *kelpie*, or water-horse, often seen by the shepherd, as he sat in a summer's evening, upon the brow of a rock, dashing along the surface of the deep, or browsing on the pasture ground, on its verge. Often did this malignant genius of the waters allure women and children to his subaqueous haunts, there to be immediately devoured. A most disastrous event of this kind is still current in tradition concerning the water-horse of Lochvenachar. Often did he also swell the torrent or lake, beyond its usual limits, to overwhelm the hapless traveller in the flood."— Graham's *Sketches descriptive of Picturesque Scenery on the Southern Confines of Perthshire.* Edin., 1806. Pp. 103-105.*

NOTE B, p. 14.

LOCH KETTERIN.

"The etymology, and consequently the spelling, of this name is so often mistaken that it may as well be rectified. *Cath-earn*, the *th* being dormant, men of war, or soldiers. Hence, following the orthography, Caterans, Ketterins; the Quatrani of Fordun. Kernes, which follows the Gaelic pronunciation, is the well-known appellation of the High-

---

* According to a later authority, the water-horse and kelpie are two distinct animals: the former haunts lochs, the latter streams and torrents. See Campbell's *Superstitions of the Highlands and Islands of Scotland.* Glasgow, 1900. P. 215.—J. S.

land freebooters as used by Shakspeare, of which this lake, from its vicinity to the Lowlands and the security of its trackless recesses, was a favourite stronghold. Hence the obvious impropriety of Loch Catherine."—Macculloch's *Description of the Western Islands of Scotland*, vol. i. Lond., 1819. P. 155.

NOTE C, p. 15.

Mrs Murray of Kensington.

The Hon. Mrs Sarah Murray, afterwards Aust, author of *A Companion and Useful Guide to the Beauties of Scotland, to the Lakes of Westmoreland, Cumberland, and Lancashire, and to the Curiosities in the District of Craven.* 8vo. Lond., 1799. In the third edition of this work, published in 1810, the author gives in the second volume an account of another tour in the Western Highlands during the summer of 1800, in which she refers to her meeting with Leyden at Loch Katrine. Though the "three active pedestrians" are not named, Leyden and his two young German friends were evidently referred to. She says (pp. 114, 115): "My friend and I had not walked a hundred yards on Loch Catherine's side, before we saw behind us three active pedestrians, skipping amongst the rocks, with hammers in their hands, striking here and there for curiosities. It was not long before they joined us; and, like sojourners in a distant land, we greeted each other with pleasure and freedom. The eldest was a clergyman, accompanying two sprightly youths through the Highlands. They had a horse for their baggage, and one between the three gentlemen to ride on alternately. The youngest had thus early in his journey gotten his foot sadly cut by scrambling amongst the rocks, but his ardent spirit made him think lightly of his wound. Upon looking at his face I discovered his name, for he bore such a strong resemblance to his brother that I could not be mistaken. His brother was one of the German gentlemen whom I met in Glen Croe in the year 1796. It was singular enough that I should, at the distance of four years, meet another of the same family equally accidentally, and in fully as wild a region. My friend and I were, after viewing Loch Catherine, to return to Callender; the gentlemen were on their way to the foot of Ben Lomond, whose lofty summit they meant to gain the next day."

NOTE D, p. 70.

Mountain of Scarba.

Sir Walter Scott visited the scenery here described in 1814 — three years after Leyden's death ; and in *The Lord of the Isles*, published the following year, he pays a beautiful tribute to the memory of his friend :—

> "Scarba's isle, whose tortured shore
> Still rings to Corrievreken's roar,
>   And lonely Colonsay ;
> —Scenes sung by him who sings no more !
> His bright and brief career is o'er,
>   And mute' his tuneful strains ;
> Quench'd is his lamp of varied lore,
> That loved the light of song to pour ;—
> A distant and a deadly shore
>   Has Leyden's cold remains !".
>   —Canto iv., stanza 11.

NOTE E, p. 102.

Rev. Donald MacNicol.

The Rev. Donald MacNicol, an eminent Gaelic scholar and antiquary, was minister of Lismore in Argyleshire, and author of *Remarks on Dr Samuel Johnson's Journey to the Hebrides ; in which are contained, Observations on the Antiquities, Language, Genius, and Manners of the Highlanders of Scotland*. 8vo. Lond., 1779. This is a severe and somewhat scurrilous criticism of Dr Johnson's *Tour to the Hebrides*. After reading the work, the great lexicographer remarked to a friend, "Really these Highland *savages* write the English language wonderfully well ! "

NOTE F, p. 257.

Bruar Water.

"It was the wish of the Duke [of Atholl] that Burns should visit the banks of the Bruar, where the scenery is bold and naked. The Poet, accustomed to the wooded banks of the Ayr and the Doon, was not disposed to admire the barren sublimity of the Bruar, and accordingly wrote a rhyming petition, in which the water requests the umbrage of birch and hazel from the hands of the noble proprietor. This was almost the only wish which the Poet ever uttered that any pains were taken to gratify. The banks of the Bruar are now clothed as he prescribed,—the trouts are sheltered from the sun by the overhanging boughs — the songster's nest is to be seen in its season,

> 'And birks extend their fragrant arms
> To screen the dear embrace.'"

—*The Life of Robert Burns.* By Allan Cunningham. Lond., 1835. P. 172.

BIBLIOGRAPHY

OF

THE LIFE AND WRITINGS OF

DR JOHN LEYDEN

I.	POETICAL WORKS	287
II.	PROSE WORKS AND TRANSLATIONS	291
III.	BIOGRAPHY, CRITICISM, ETC.	295
IV.	MANUSCRIPTS	310

BIBLIOGRAPHY.

I. POETICAL WORKS.

Scenes of Infancy: Descriptive of Teviotdale. By John Leyden. 12mo. Edinburgh, 1803.

    'The Vale of Teviot' was the original title given to this work, and it was announced in 'The Scots Magazine' for June 1802 as about to be published under that title, but Leyden afterwards altered it to 'Scenes of Infancy.'

Scenes of Infancy: Descriptive of Teviotdale. By John Leyden. Second edition, 12mo. Edinburgh, 1811.

The Poetical Remains of the late Dr John Leyden. With Memoir of his Life. By the Rev. James Morton. 8vo. London, 1819.

* Scenes of Infancy, and other Poems. By the late Dr John Leyden. With a Memoir of the Author. [By Sir Walter Scott, Bart.] 18mo. Jedburgh, 1844.

    Dedicated to Mr Andrew Leyden, Farmer, Roundhaugh, Roxburghshire, Dr Leyden's youngest brother.

* Poems and Ballads. By Dr John Leyden. With a Memoir of the Author by Sir Walter Scott, Bart.,

---

* A portion of the material of the Rev. James Morton's Memoir of Leyden is embodied in the editions marked with asterisks.

and Supplement by Robert White. Cr. 8vo. Kelso, 1858.

*Poems and Ballads. By Dr John Leyden. With a Memoir of the Author by Sir Walter Scott, Bart., and Supplementary Memoir [by Robert White]. Cr. 8vo. Kelso, 1875.

The Poetical Works of Dr John Leyden. With Memoir by Thomas Brown, and Portrait from the Original Pencil Sketch by Captain Elliot. Cr. 8vo. Edinburgh, 1875.

Scenes of Infancy: Descriptive of Teviotdale. By John Leyden, M.D. With a Biographical Sketch of the Author by the Rev. W. W. Tulloch, B.D. 12mo. Kelso, 1875.

Scenes of Infancy. By Dr John Leyden. 18mo. Edinburgh. *N.D.*

This edition, though issued separately in paper covers, forms part of a volume entitled 'Poems of Graham, Blair, Beattie, Gray, and Leyden.' Edin. *N.D.*

Edinburgh Magazine, The, or Literary Miscellany. New Series. Edin., 1795-1799.

Vol. 5—
Danish Ode, pp. 301, 302.
Elegiac Lines, pp. 302, 303.
The Fairy, pp. 303, 304.

Vol. 6—
Bellicosum Facinus, or the Doughty Deed, pp. 383, 384.
Flaminius ad Agellum Suum, imitated, pp. 222, 223.
Robertslaw [Ruberslaw], pp. 219-222.
The Descent of Odin, Part I. omitted by Gray, p. 222.
The Incantation of Hervor: A Runic Ode. From Olaus Verilius. Pp. 382, 383.

Vol. 7—
Anacreontic, p. 60.
Moonlight, p. 60.
Ode to the Scenes of Infancy, pp. 59, 60.

Vol. 11—
Amorite War Ode. From the Hebrew. Pp. 465, 466.
Ode to Phantasy, pp. 302-304.

Edinburgh Magazine, The (*continued*).
   Vol. 11 (*continued*)—
      Ode to Spring. A Fragment from the Ethiopic. P. 467.
      Ode to Spring. From Ibycus. P. 467.
      Ode to Spring. From Meleager. P. 467.
      Ode to Virtue. From Aristotle. P. 466.
      Sonnet. From the Italian of Michelangelo Buonaroti. P. 467.
      Spartan War Ode. From Tyrtæus. P. 466.
      The Arab Warrior. From the Arabic of Hariri. P. 466.
      The Cretan Warrior. From Hybrias of Crete. P. 466.
      The Shepherd's Wish. From the Greek of Moschus. P. 304.
      The Wail of Danae. From the Greek of Simonides. Pp. 304, 305.
      Timur's War Song. From the Persic of Ali Yezdi. P. 466.
   Vol. 12—
      Revenge: An Ode. Pp. 140, 141.
      The Dryad's Warning. To Robert Anderson, M.D., on an Excursion in the Country. Pp. 60, 61.
   Vol. 13—
      Elegy on the Death of a Favourite Linnet. Addressed to Miss A——n. Pp. 301, 302.

Scots Magazine, The, 1801 and 1802. Edin., 1801-2.
   Vol. 63—
      The Three Pots; or, Æsop Realised. P. 120.
   Vol. 64—
      Chinese Ode. From Bayer's Latin version. P. 345.
      Epistle to Almira, from a "Dancing Bear," pp. 693, 694.
      Fragment of the Nidi Woupi: A Tamulic Poem. From the Latin of Bayer. P. 694.
      Hungarian War-Song, pp. 162, 163.
      Ode to Jehovah. From the Hebrew of Moses. Pp. 344, 345.
      The Dream: addressed to W. Drummond of Hawthornden. From the Latin of J. Leoch. Pp. 692, 693.
      The Green Veil, sent to a Lady with Hammond's Poems, pp. 591, 592.
      The Monody of Tograi. From the Arabic. Pp. 255-257.

Lewis, M. G. Tales of Wonder; Written and Collected by. Vol. i. Lond., 1801.
   The Elfin-King, pp. 214-225.

Scott, Sir Walter, Bart. Minstrelsy of the Scottish Border. 3 vols. Kelso and Edin., 1802-3.
> *Vol. 1—*
> Ode on Visiting Flodden, pp. 252-258.
>
> *Vol. 2—*
> Lord Soulis, pp. 327-354.
> Scotish Music, an Ode, pp. 1-6.
> The Cout of Keeldar, pp. 355-372.
>
> *Vol. 3—*
> The Mermaid, pp. 297-320.

Macleay, K., M.D. Description of the Spar Cave, lately discovered in the Isle of Skye, &c. Edin., 1811.
> The Mermaid, pp. 77-88. In this copy four additional stanzas appear, two are omitted, and some freedom has been used with a few of the verses.

Spy, The : A Periodical Paper of Literary Amusement and Instruction. [Edited by James Hogg.] Edin., 1811.
> Song of Wallace, p. 168.

A Memorial of Anne Margaret Anderson, the wife of David Irving, LL.D. Edin., 1813.
> Elegy on the Death of a Favourite Linnet, addressed to Miss Anderson. By the late John Leyden, M.D., Professor of Hindostanee in the College of Fort-William. Pp. 9, 10. First published in 'The Edinburgh Magazine,' April 1799. Pp. 301, 302.

Brydges, Sir Egerton, Bart. Restituta ; or, Titles, Extracts, and Characters of Old Books in English Literature Revived. Vol. iv. Lond., 1816.
> Lai of the Ettercap, pp. 212-215.

Lewis, M. G., The Life and Correspondence of. 2 vols. Lond., 1839.
> Contains an account of Dr Leyden, and verses by him addressed to Miss Sophia Lewis not published in any edition of his poems. Vol. i. pp. 31-38 ; vol. ii. p. 50.

Froude, James Anthony, M.A. Thomas Carlyle: A History of the first Forty Years of his Life, 1795-1835. Vol. i. Lond., 1882.
> Verses to Mrs Buller on seeing her in a Highland Dress. By Doctor John Leyden. P. 167, note.

Drummond's Polemo-Middinia, Translation of the opening passage in. [By John Leyden.] MS.
> For bringing under my notice this interesting fragment of the opening stanzas of Leyden's translation of this poem, I am indebted to Mr A. H. Millar, Dundee. The verses do not seem ever to have been published.—J. S.

II. PROSE WORKS AND TRANSLATIONS.

A Historical and Philosophical Sketch of the Discoveries and Settlements of the Europeans in Northern and Western Africa at the close of the Eighteenth Century. [By John Leyden.] Fcap. 8vo. Edinburgh, 1799.

Historische und Philosophische Skizze der Entdeckungen et Niederlassungen der Europaer in Nord und West Africa, um ende der achtzehnten Jahrhunderts. Aus dem Engl. von S. St. 8vo. Bremen, 1802.
> German translation of the preceding.

The Complaynt of Scotland. Written in 1548. With a Preliminary Dissertation and Glossary. [By J. Leyden.] 8vo. Edinburgh, 1801.
> Large paper edition. 4to. Edinburgh, 1801.
>> A dedication (2 pp. 8vo) to Richard Heber, Esq., differing from the one published, and which I believe was never issued, is in the possession of Mr Macmath, and presumably the only copy in existence. It formerly belonged to Mr David Laing.—J. S.

Observations on the 'Complaynt of Scotland.' 8vo. Edin., 1802.

Scots Magazine, The, 1795, 1801, and 1802. Edin., 1795, 1801-2.

   Vol. 57—
      Strictures upon the Ancient Scottish Language, pp. 164-166.

   Vol. 63—
      On Misanthropy, pp. 243-246.

   Vol. 64—
      Notice of an Edition of Drummond of Hawthornden's Works, pp. 714, 715.
      Observations on the 'Complaynt of Scotland,' pp. 566-573.
      On the Authenticity of Ossian's Poems, pp. 39, 40.
      On the Carrier Dove, pp. 226, 227.
      Specimens of the Poetry of St Kilda, pp. 976, 977.
      Strictures on Mr Laing's Dissertation on the Poems of Ossian, pp. 541-545, 647-652, 733-738, 797-805, 873-881, 966-973.

Scott, Sir Walter, Bart. Minstrelsy of the Scottish Border. Vol. ii. Kelso, 1802.

   Essay on the Fairies of Popular Superstition. Introduction to 'The Young Tamlane.' Pp. 167-227.

Scotish Descriptive Poems. With some Illustrations of Scotish Literary Antiquities. (Containing John Wilson's 'Clyde,' 2 parts; 'Albania' (anonymous); Alexander Hume's 'Day Estival'; William Fowler's Poems.) [By John Leyden.] 12mo. Edinburgh, 1803.

* Dissertation on the Languages and Literature of the Indo-Chinese Nations. By John Leyden, M.D. Royal 4to. Calcutta, 1808.

   Reprinted in 'Miscellaneous Papers relating to Indo-China,' vol. i. (Trübner's Oriental Series); Lond., 1866; pp. 84-171. With Notes by the Editor [Dr Reinhold Rost].

* The Rosheniah Sect and its Founder, Báyezid Ansárí. By John Leyden, M.D. Royal 4to. Calcutta, 1810.

---

   * These appear to have been issued in a separate form from the Calcutta edition of the 'Asiatic Researches.'

A Comparative Vocabulary of the Barma, Maláyu, and T'hái Languages. [By John Leyden.] 8vo. Serampore, 1810.

British and Foreign Bible Society, Report of The. May 1, 1811.

In the above report it is stated that Dr Leyden had engaged to translate certain books of the New Testament into the following languages: The Siamese, Macassar, Bugis, Afghan, Rakheng, Maldivian, and Jaghatai. This engagement was partly fulfilled, the following gospels in manuscript having in little more than a year from the first proposal been delivered to the secretary:—
  1. Pushtu—Matthew's Gospel; Mark's Gospel.
  2. Maldivian—The Four Gospels.
  3. Baloch—Mark's Gospel.
  4. Macassar—Mark's Gospel.
  5. Bugis—Mark's Gospel.

Asiatic Researches; or, Transactions of the Society instituted in Bengal for Inquiry into the History and Antiquities, the Arts, Sciences, and Literature of Asia. Vols. x. and xi. Lond., 1811-12.

On the Languages and Literature of the Indo-Chinese Nations. By J. Leyden, M.D. Vol. x. pp. 158-289.

On the Rosheniah Sect and its Founder, Báyezid Ansári. By J. Leyden, M.D. Vol. xi. pp. 363-428.

Batavian Society of Arts and Sciences, Transactions of the. Vol. vii. 8vo. Batavia, 1814.

Sketch of Borneo. By the late Dr Leyden. 64 pp.

Historical Account of Discoveries and Travels in Africa. By the late John Leyden, M.D. Enlarged, and completed to the present time, &c., by Hugh Murray, Esq., F.R.S.E. 2 vols. 8vo. Edinburgh, 1817.

Second edition. 2 vols. 8vo. Edinburgh, 1818.

Malay Annals. Translated from the Malay Language by the late Dr John Leyden. With an Introduction by Sir Thomas Stamford Raffles, F.R.S. 8vo. London, 1821.

Memoirs of Zehir-ed-din Muhammed Baber, Emperor of Hindustan. Written by himself in the Jaghatai Turki, and translated, partly by the late John Leyden, Esq., M.D., partly by William Erskine, Esq. With Notes and a Geographical and Historical Introduction. 4to. London, 1826.

The Life of Baber, Emperor of Hindostan. By R. M. Caldecott, Esq. 8vo. London, 1844.

> Inscribed to the Memory of John Leyden, M.D. An abridgment of the preceding.

Muhammad Bāba(Zahīr-al-dīn), Emperor of Hindostan. Denkwürdigkeiten des Zehir-Eddin Muhammed Baber . . . nach der englischen Uebersetzung des Dr Leyden und W. Erskine deutsch bearbeitet, &c. 8vo. Leipzig, 1828.

Literary Gems. [Edited by James Shaw.] Edin., 1826.

> The Edinburgh Booksellers (1802). By Dr Leyden. Pp. 54-61. Originally published in 'The Scots Magazine,' November 1803, and reprinted in the appendix to 'Letters from Bishop Percy, &c., to George Paton.' Edin., 1830.

Critiques by Mr David Herd and others upon the new edition of 'The Complaynt of Scotland.' With Observations in answer by the Editor, the late Dr John Leyden. 8vo. Edin., 1829.

> Large paper edition. 4to. Edin., 1829.

Wilson, John. Clyde: A Descriptive Poem. With Life of the Author by John Leyden, M.D. 8vo. Lond., 1852.

> Another edition. 8vo. Lond., 1859.
> Another edition. 8vo. Lond. *N.D.*

Journal of a Tour in the Highlands and Western Islands of Scotland in 1800. By John Leyden. Cr. 8vo. Edinburgh, 1903.

> Large paper edition. 4to. Edinburgh, 1903. (*Only 25 copies printed.*)

III. BIOGRAPHY, CRITICISM, Etc.

All the Year Round. A Weekly Journal conducted by Charles Dickens. New Series. Vol. xxxviii. Lond., 1886.
> John Leyden, the Poet, pp. 251, 252.

Allan, George. Life of Sir Walter Scott, Bart. With Critical Notices of his Writings. Edin., 1834.
> John Leyden, pp. 192-195, 214, 215, 382.

Allibone, S. Austin. Critical Dictionary of English Literature, &c. Vol. ii. Lond., 1870.
> John Leyden, M.D. (1775-1811), p. 1095.

Anderson, John. History of Edinburgh. Edin., 1856.
> John Leyden, p. 316.

Anderson, William. The Popular Scotish Biography, &c. Edin., 1842.
> John Leyden, M.D., pp. 497, 498.

Anderson, William. The Scottish Nation, &c. Vol. ii. Edin., 1865.
> John Leyden, M.D., pp. 664, 665.

Anecdotes of Books and Authors. Lond., 1836.
> Leyden, pp. 133, 134.

Annual Register, The, 1812. Lond., 1813.
> Doctor Leyden, pp. 457-461.

Antiquaries of Scotland, Proceedings of the Society of. Vol. xxxv. Edin., 1901.
> Note on Dr John Leyden's MS. 'Journal of a Tour in the Highlands, Western Isles, and other parts of Scotland in 1800.' By Sir Arthur Mitchell, K.C.B., M.D., LL.D. P. 529.

Ballantyne, Mrs John. Rambling Reminiscences of Sir Walter Scott and some of his Friends. Chambers's Edinburgh Journal. Vol. xii. Edin., 1844.
    Anecdote of Leyden, p. 333.

Berwickshire Naturalist Club, History of the, 1876-1878. Alnwick, 1879.
    Anecdotes of Dr John Leyden, pp. 427, 428, 472.

Blackwood's Edinburgh Magazine. Vol. v. Edin., 1819.
    Dr Leyden, Poetical Remains of, pp. 3-8.

Bonar, Rev. Andrew R. The Poets and Poetry of Scotland. Edin., 1864.
    John Leyden, pp. 285-290.

Border Counties Magazine, The. Vol. i. Galashiels, 1880.
    Border Biography, "John Leyden," pp. 217-220, 241-245.

Border Magazine, The. Edited by Nicholas Dickson. Vol. i. Glasgow, 1896.
    Note respecting the Discovery of a Portrait of John Leyden, painted by Sir David Wilkie, p. 39.
    Dr John Leyden's Indian Career, pp. 133-136.

Border Treasury, The, of Things New and Old. Galashiels, 1874-5.
    Letters to the Editor on Portrait of Dr Leyden. By T. L , p. 296; J. and J. H Rutherfurd, pp. 305, 306; Robert Murray, p. 306 ; Wm. Brockie, p. 306.

Bower, Alexander. History of the University of Edinburgh. Vol. iii. Edin., 1830.
    Dr John Leyden, pp. 309, 311-313, 340.

British Critic, The. Vol. xx. Lond., 1802.
    Leyden's 'Complaynt of Scotland,' pp. 8-13.

Brown, Thomas, M.D., Account of the Life and Writings of. By Rev. David Welsh. Edin., 1825.
> Leyden, pp. 29, 77, 499, 501-503.

Browne, Rev. George. History of the British and Foreign Bible Society. Vol. ii. Lond., 1859.
> Dr Leyden, pp. 109, 112.

Brydges, Sir Egerton, Bart. Restituta; or, Titles, Extracts, and Characters of Old Books in English Literature Revived. Vol. iii. Lond., 1815.
> Leyden's Scotish Descriptive Poems, pp. 132, 133.

Calcutta Review, The. Vol. xxxi. Calcutta, 1858.
> John Leyden, pp. 1-53.

Campbell, Thomas, Life and Letters of. Edited by William Beattie, M.D. 3 vols. Lond., 1850.
> John Leyden, vol. i. pp. 243-246; vol. iii. p. 253.

Carre, Walter Riddell. Border Memories; or, Sketches of Prominent Men and Women of the Border. Edin., 1876.
> Dr John Leyden, pp. 253-256.

Catalogue of the Scott Centenary Exhibition held at Edinburgh in 1871. Edin., 1872.
> Letter of Sir Walter Scott, addressed "Dr Leyden, Calcutta," pp. 155, 156. It has a pathetic interest as being the last letter Scott wrote to Leyden, and was returned unopened.

Cates, William L. R. A Dictionary of General Biography. Fourth edition. Lond., 1885.
> John Leyden, p. 757.

Chalmers, Thomas, D.D., LL.D., Memoirs of the Life

and Writings of. By Rev. Wm. Hanna, LL.D. Vol. i. Edin., 1850.

John Leyden, pp. 22, 48, 49. Letter from, pp. 461, 462. Feud between Leyden and Campbell—Notice of 'The Clerical Review,' by Dr Irving, pp. 467-469.

Chambers's Biographical Dictionary. Edited by David Patrick, LL.D., and Francis Hindes Groome. Edin., 1897.

John Leyden, p. 589.

Chambers's Cyclopædia of English Literature, &c. Third edition. Vol. ii. Edin., 1876.

John Leyden, pp. 39-41.

Chambers's Edinburgh Journal. Vol. iii. Edin., 1835.

Biographic Sketches, "John Leyden," pp. 261-263. Republished in 'Chambers's Miscellany of Instructive and Entertaining Tracts.'

Chambers's Encyclopædia : A Dictionary of Universal Knowledge. New edition. Vol. vi. Edin., 1890.

John Leyden, p. 601.

Chambers, Robert. Biographical Dictionary of Eminent Scotsmen. New edition. Vol. iii. Glasgow, 1855.

John Leyden, pp. 426-446.

Chambers, Robert, LL.D. Life of Sir Walter Scott. With Abbotsford Notanda by Robert Carruthers, LL.D. Edin., 1871.

John Leyden, pp. 43, 115, 120, 123, 125.

Cockburn, Henry. Memorials of his Time. Edin., 1856.

John Leyden, pp. 178-181.

Colton, Rev. C. C., A.M. Lacon ; or, Many Things in Few Words. Vol. ii. Lond., 1822.

Note on Doctor Leyden's Ode to an Indian Gold Coin, pp. 98, 99.

Constable, Archibald, and his Literary Correspondents. By his Son, Thomas Constable. Vol. i. Edin., 1873.
> John Leyden, pp. 190-212; Letters of Alexander Murray with reference to, pp. 308 *et seq.*; Biographical Notice of, by Sir Walter Scott, pp. 312, 313.

Craig, R. S. In Borderland. Border and other Verses. Hawick, 1899.
> To John Leyden, pp. 61, 62.

Critical Review, The; or, Annals of Literature. Vol. xxxv. Lond., 1802.
> Leyden's edition of 'The Complaynt of Scotland,' pp. 95-99.

Crockett, W. S., Minister of Tweedsmuir. In Praise of Tweed. Selkirk, 1899.
> John Leyden, pp. 52-54.

Crockett, W. S., Minister of Tweedsmuir. The Scott Country. Lond., 1902.
> The Land of Leyden, pp. 100-117.

Cyclopædia of Biography. Conducted by Charles Knight. Vol. iii. Lond., 1858.
> John Leyden, M.D., p. 875.

Dawson, James Hooper. An Abridged Statistical History of Scotland. Edin., 1853.
> Leyden, Poet and Linguist, pp. 914, 915.

Dickson, Robert, and Edmond, John P. Annals of Scottish Printing. Cambridge, 1890.
> John Leyden, on date of Bellenden's 'Croniklis,' p. 131; edits 'Complaynt of Scotland,' pp. 137-149.

Dictionary of National Biography. Edited by Sidney Lee. Vol. xxxiii. Lond., 1893.
> John Leyden, M.D. (1775-1811), pp. 215, 216.

Dodds, Rev. James. Personal Reminiscences and Biographical Sketches. Second edition. Edin., 1888.
> Dr John Leyden, pp. 199-213.

Douglas, Sir George, Bart. A History of the Border Counties. Edin., 1899.
> Leyden, pp. 102, 427, 428, 438, 446, 450.

Drake, Nathan, M.D. Winter Nights; or, Fire-side Lucubrations. Vol. i. Lond., 1820.
> Critical Observations on 'Scenes of Infancy: a Poem,' by Dr Leyden, pp. 77-146.

Duncan, Rev. Henry, D.D., Ruthwell. Memoir of the. By his Son, Rev. George J. C. Duncan. Edin., 1848.
> Valuable and curious MSS. of Dr John Leyden, pp. 147, 148.

Edinburgh Annual Register, The, for 1811. Vol. iv. 2 parts. Edin., 1813.
> Notice of John Leyden. Part i. p. 209.
> Biographical Memoir of. [By Sir Walter Scott, Bart.] Part ii. pp. xli-lxviii. Republished in his Miscellaneous Prose Works.
> Verses to the memory of Leyden. [By Sir John Malcolm.] Pp. xci, xcii.

Edinburgh Encyclopædia, The. Conducted by David Brewster, LL.D. Vol. xii. Edin., 1830.
> John Leyden, pp. 719, 720.

Egerton, Hugh Edward, M.A. Sir Stamford Raffles. England in the Far East. Lond., 1900.
> Dr John Leyden, pp. 9, 18-20, 25, 47-49, 58.

Elliot, The Hon. George F. S. The Border Elliots and the Family of Minto. Edin. (*Privately printed*.) 1897.
> Leyden, p. 83.

Encyclopædia Britannica. Ninth edition. Vol. xiv. Edin., 1882.
> John Leyden, M.D. (1775-1811), pp. 495, 496.

Gallovidian, The. Vol. iv. Dumfries, 1902.
> Was John Leyden the Prototype of Dominie Sampson? By John Reith, B.D. Pp. 171-179.

Galt, John, The Literary Life and Miscellanies of. Vol. i. Edin., 1834.
> Dr Leyden, pp. 28, 29.

Gentleman's Magazine, The, and Historical Chronicle, vols. lxxxi. and lxxxii. Lond., 1811-12.
> Dr Leyden, Notice of his Death, vol. lxxxi. part ii. pp. 658, 659; Dr Leyden, Poetry of, vol. lxxxii. part i. pp. 409-411; Leyden's Translation of Strabo, p. 420; Memoirs of, p. 486; Dr Leyden's Oriental Library, part ii. p. 240.

Gilfillan, Rev. George. Life of Sir Walter Scott, Bart. Second edition. Edin., 1871.
> John Leyden, pp. 50-52.

[Gillies, R. P.] Recollections of Sir Walter Scott, Bart. Lond., 1837.
> John Leyden, pp. 111-119, 151.

Good Words. Edited by the Very Rev. Donald Macleod, D.D. Lond., 1897.
> Anecdotes of Leyden, p. 564.

Graham, Henry Grey. Scottish Men of Letters in the Eighteenth Century. Lond., 1901.
> John Leyden, p. 435.

Haig, James. A Topographical and Historical Account of the Town of Kelso. Edin., 1825.
> John Leyden, M.D., pp. 305-310.

Hawick Archæological Society, Transactions of the. Hawick, 1867, 1875.
> The Poet Leyden. By Robert Murray. 1867. Pp. 15-17.
> Traditions and Recollections of Dr John Leyden. By James Douglas of Cavers. 1875.

Herens, James L. Songs of the Borderland. Kelso. *N.D.*
    Dr John Leyden, pp. 132-134.

Hogg's Weekly Instructor. New Series. Vol. ii. Edin., 1849.
    John Leyden, M.D., pp. 142-144.

Irving, Joseph. The Book of Scotsmen, &c. Paisley, 1881.
    John Leyden, M.D., Poet and Linguist, p. 274.

Jeffrey, Alexander. The History and Antiquities of Roxburghshire. Vol. iv. Edin., 1864.
    John Leyden, pp. 361-364.

Jeffrey, Francis, Lord. Contributions to the Edinburgh Review. Second edition. Vol. i. Lond., 1846.
    Review of Leyden and Erskine's Memoirs of Baber, pp. 719-755.

Jerdan, William, The Autobiography of. Vol. i. Lond., 1852.
    Similarity of the History of Thomson and Leyden, pp. 218, 219.

Keble, Rev. J., M.A. Miscellaneous Poems. Second edition. Oxford, 1869.
    To the Memory of John Leyden, M.D., pp. 180, 181.

Laidlaw, Walter. Poetry and Prose. [Kelso, 1900.]
    Dr John Leyden, pp. 78-82.

Leisure Hour, The. Lond., 1875.
    Dr John Leyden, pp. 604-608.

Letters from Joseph Ritson, Esq., to Mr George Paton, &c. Edin., 1829.
    Leyden's 'Complaynt of Scotland,' p. 16.

BIBLIOGRAPHY 303

Lives of Scottish Poets. By the Society of Ancien Scots. 6 parts. Lond., 1822.

> Dr John Leyden. Part ii. pp. 36, 40, 52; Part iii. p. 94; Part iv. pp. 18, 31; Part v. p. 172; Part vi. pp. 136-143.

Lockhart, J. G. Memoirs of the Life of Sir Walter Scott, Bart. 7 vols. Edin., 1837-8.

> Dr John Leyden. Vol. i. pp. 66, 67, 322, 333, 344, 359 368, 370, 405. Vol. ii. pp. 80, 92, 197, 216, 371-375. Vol. iii. p. 264. Vol. vi. p. 326.

Lockhart, J. G. The Life of Sir Walter Scott. Vol. iii. Edin.: T. C. & E. C. Jack. 1902.

> John Leyden, M.D., Portrait of, by Captain Elliot, facing p. 296. Interesting Note respecting same [by James L. Caw, F.S.A. Scot.], p. xii.

MacFarlane, Charles. Our Indian Empire. Vol. ii. Lond., 1847.

> Death of Dr John Leyden, pp. 187, 188, note.

Mackintosh, Sir James, Memoirs of the Life of. Edited by his Son. Vol. i. Lond., 1836.

> Dr Leyden, his philological researches, p. 240.

Marshman, John Clark. The Life and Times of Carey, Marshman, and Ward. 2 vols. Lond., 1859.

> Dr Leyden, vol. i. pp. 321-323, 389, 390, 425, 434-436, 438, 449-451; vol. ii. pp. 186, 333, 335.

Maunder, Samuel. Select British Biography, &c. Lond., 1839.

> John Leyden, p. 182.

Maunder, Samuel. The Biographical Treasury, &c. Sixth edition. Lond., 1847.

> John Leyden, p. 500.

Mezzofanti, Cardinal, The Life of. With an Introductory Memoir of Eminent Linguists, Ancient and Modern. By C. W. Russell, D.D. Lond., 1858.
    John Leyden, pp. 91, 92.

Mitchell, James, LL.D. The Scotsman's Library, &c. Edin., 1825.
    Dr Leyden, pp. 141-143.

Moir, D. M. Sketches of the Poetical Literature of the Past Half Century. Edin., 1851.
    John Leyden, pp. 34-36.

Monthly Review; or Literary Journal. Vol. xci. Lond., 1820.
    Dr Leyden, Poetical Remains of, pp. 61-68.

Morehead, Rev. Robert, D.D., Memorials of the Life and Writings of. Edited by his Son. Edin., 1875.
    Dr John Leyden, pp. 103, 174.

Morton, Rev. James. Memoirs of the Life and Writings of the Celebrated Literary Character, the late Dr John Leyden, of the Honourable East India Company's Establishment. 18mo. Calcutta, 1825.

Murray, Alexander, D.D. History of the European Languages, &c. With a Life of the Author. Vol. i. Edin., 1823.
    Dr John Leyden, pp. lxxii-lxxv, lxxix-lxxxii, cxv, cxviii, cxix, 176, 186.

Murray, Robert. Hawick Songs and Song Writers. Third edition. Hawick, 1897.
    Dr John Leyden, pp. 4, 5.

Murray, Robert. History of Hawick from the Earliest Times to 1832. Hawick, 1901.
    Dr Leyden, pp. 70, 71.

Napier, George G. The Homes and Haunts of Sir Walter Scott, Bart. Glasgow, 1897.
>Dr John Leyden, pp. 6, 7, 57-62, 70, 138.

New Scots Magazine, The. Edin., 1828-29.
>Memorials of Dr John Leyden, vol. i. pp. 73-78, 111-120.
>Anecdotes of Dr Leyden, vol. ii. pp. 98-104.

New Statistical Account of Scotland. Roxburghshire. Edin., 1841.
>Dr John Leyden, pp. 377, 432.

Notes and Queries: A Medium of Inter-Communication for Literary Men, &c. Second and Seventh Series. Lond., 1859-60, 1887.
>*Second Series*, vol. 7—
>>Portrait of Leyden. By J. Mn. P. 236.
>>Dr John Leyden. By C. B. Pp. 384, 385.
>>Dr John Leyden. By E. H. A. P. 443.
>>Dr John Leyden. By J. P. 443.
>
>*Second Series*, vol. 9—
>>John Leyden. By T. P. 385.
>
>*Seventh Series*, vol. 4—
>>Dr John *Caspar* Leyden, his Christian Name. By J. C. Goodfellow. P. 484.

Oliphant, Mrs. The Literary History of England. Vol. ii. Lond., 1882.
>John Leyden, pp. 101-107, 188.

Owen, Rev. John, A.M. The History of the Origin and First Ten Years of the British and Foreign Bible Society. Vol. ii. Lond., 1816.
>Dr Leyden, pp. 35, 36, 252, 255, 256.

Penny Cyclopædia, The, of the Society for Diffusion of Useful Knowledge. Vol. xiii. Lond., 1839.
>John Leyden, M.D., p. 457.

Popular Encyclopædia, The ; or, Conversations Lexicon. Vol. iv. Glasgow, 1844.
> John Leyden, p. 456.

Raffles, Sir Stamford, The Life of. By Demetrius Charles Boulger. Lond., 1897.
> Contains an interesting account of Leyden's Indian career. Pp. 'xiii, xiv, 13, 18-21, 36-42, 79, 93, 94, 97, 98, 128, 131-133, 159, 184.

Raffles, Sir Thomas Stamford, F.R.S., Memoir of the Life and Public Services of. Vol. i. Lond., 1835.
> Letters from Dr Leyden, pp. 41, 42, 48, 49, 51-53. Death of, p. 131.

Raffles, Thomas Stamford. The History of Java. 2 vols. Lond., 1817.
> Dr Leyden, vol. i. p. x ; vol. ii. pp. clxi, clxxxviii.

Ritson, Joseph, The Letters of. With Memoir of the Author. By Sir Harris Nicolas. 2 vols. Lond., 1833.
> Dr Leyden, vol. i. pp. lx, lxxi; vol. ii. pp. 226, 229, 238, 240.

Rogers, Charles, D.D., LL.D. Social Life in Scotland, &c. Vol. iii. Edin., 1886.
> Dr John Leyden, pp. 48, 49, 257, 258.

Rogers, Charles, LL.D. The Modern Scottish Minstrel, &c. Vol. ii. Edin., 1856.
> John Leyden, M.D., pp. 191-198.

Rose, Rev. H. J. A New General Biographical Dictionary. Vol. ix. Lond., 1848.
> John Leyden, pp. 263, 264.

Ross, J. The Book of Scottish Poems : Ancient and Modern. With Memoirs of the Authors. Edin., 1878.
> John Leyden, 1775-1811, pp. 713-721.

Russell, James, D.D. Reminiscences of Yarrow. Edin., 1886.
: Dr Leyden's Misadventure, pp. 205, 206.

Rutherfurd's Border Hand-Book. Kelso, 1849.
: Dr John Leyden, pp. 46, 47, 63, 73.

Scots Magazine, The, 1802. Vol. lxiv. Edin., 1802.
: On the 'Complaynt of Scotland,' by D[avid] H[erd], p. 51.

Scot, David, M.D., Minister of Corstorphine. Essays on various Subjects of Belles Lettres. Edin., 1824.
: On the Life and Poetry of Leyden, pp. 175-196.

Scott, Sir Walter, Familiar Letters of. 2 vols. Edin., 1894.
: Dr John Leyden, vol. i. pp. 18, 19, 72, 157, 158, 241; Letter from Scott to, pp. 33-38; Letter from Leyden to Scott, pp. 161-163; Lord Minto on Leyden's abilities, pp. 163, 164. Vol. ii., Leyden compared with Sir Wm. Jones, p. 55; Leyden, p. 259.

Scott, Sir Walter. Minstrelsy of the Scottish Border. Edited by T. F. Henderson. 4 vols. Edin., 1902.
: John Leyden, vol. i. pp. xiii, xx; vol. iv. p. 57; his connection with the Essay on Fairy Superstition, vol. i. pp. 174-176; contributions to the 'Minstrelsy,' vol. ii. pp. 293-299; vol. iii. pp. 414-420; vol. iv. pp. 218-258, 259-276, 277-301.

Scott, Sir Walter, The Journal of, from the Original Manuscript at Abbotsford. Vol. i. Edin., 1891.
: John Leyden, pp. 218, 349.

Scott, Sir Walter, Bart. The Lord of the Isles. Edin., 1815.
: Tribute to the memory of Leyden, canto iv. stanza 11.

Scottish Notes and Queries. Vol. ix. Aberdeen, 1896.
: Leyden, the Poet, p. 76.

Seward, Anna, Letters of, written between the years 1784 and 1807. Vol. vi. Edin., 1811.
> John Leyden, pp. 96-98, 217.

Sketch, The, June 22, 1898. Lond., 1898.
> The Tombs of Olive, Raffles, and John Leyden.

Smith, Rev. Sydney, Memoir of. By his Daughter, Lady Holland. Vol. i. Lond., 1855.
> Leyden, p. 31.

Spence, Elizabeth I. Letters from the North Highlands during the Summer 1816. Lond., 1817.
> The Poet Leyden, pp. 2-5.

Spy, The : A Periodical Paper of Literary Amusement and Instruction. [Edited by James Hogg.] Edin., 1811.
> Mr Shuffleton's Allegorical Survey of the Scottish Poets of the Present Day—Scott, Campbell, [Hogg], Leyden. Pp. 9-15. Letter to 'The Spy' [from Walter Scott], enclosing "The Battle of Assaye," by Leyden, p. 72.

𝕴𝖍𝖊 𝕮𝖔𝖒𝖕𝖑𝖆𝖞𝖓𝖙 𝖔𝖋 𝕾𝖈𝖔𝖙𝖑𝖆𝖓𝖉𝖊, 1549. Re-edited from the originals, with Introduction and Glossary, by James A. H. Murray. Lond. (*Early English Text Society*), 1872.
> Dr John Leyden, his edition of the 'Complaynt,' p. cxvi; criticism of, p. lxvii; Introduction quoted, pp. xxx, lxix, xci, xcv; attributes 'Complaynt' to Sir D. Lyndsay, p. cxiii.

Thomson, Rev. Thomas. A History of the Scottish People. Vol. iii. Lond. *N.D.*
> John Leyden, Poet, p. 603.

Tytler, Patrick Fraser, A Memoir of. By Rev. John W. Burgon, M.A. Lond., 1859.
> Leyden, the Poet, pp. 26, 27, 39, 40.

Veitch, Prof. John. The Feeling for Nature in Scottish Poetry. Vol. ii. Edin., 1887.
> John Leyden (1775-1811), pp. 158-182.

Veitch, Prof. John. The History and Poetry of the Scottish Border. Vol. ii. Edin., 1893.

   John Leyden, pp. 111, 112, 277-284.

Veitch, John, LL.D. The Tweed, and other Poems. Glasgow, 1875.

   Leyden, pp. 106, 107, 221, 222.

Viri Illvstres. Acad. Jacob. Sext. Scot. Reg. Anno CCC^(MO.) Edin., 1884.

   John Leyden, p. 50.

Walker, Hugh, M.A. Three Centuries of Scottish Literature. Vol. ii. Glasgow, 1893.

   John Leyden, pp. 95, 105, 106.

[Watson, Jean L.] Roxburghshire and its History. Edin., 1874.

   John Leyden, pp. 75, 76, 78, 79, 87, 88.

White, Robert. Supplement to Sir Walter Scott's Biographical Memoir of Dr John Leyden. Cr. 8vo. Kelso, 1857. (*Only 25 copies printed.*)

   Inscribed to Mr Andrew Leyden, the youngest brother of Dr John Leyden.

Williamson, Rev. Alex. Glimpses of Peebles, or Forgotten Chapters in its History. Selkirk, 1895.

   John Leyden, pp. 124, 125, 128.

Wilson, James. Hawick and its Old Memories, &c. Edin., 1858.

   Memorials of Dr John Leyden, pp. 165-178.

Wilson, James Grant. The Poets and Poetry of Scotland, 1219-1776. Lond., 1876.

   John Leyden, pp. 514-526.

Wordsworth, Dorothy. Recollections of a Tour made in Scotland, A.D. 1803. Edited by J. C. Shairp, LL.D. Second edition. Edin., 1874.
> Leyden, pp. 269, 270.

IV. MANUSCRIPTS.

LEYDEN (DR JOHN) MANUSCRIPTS.

British Museum, London.

Leyden (John), M.D., Secretary to the Asiatic Society—Translation of Baber's Commentaries.
Translations and Philological Collections of Oriental Languages.
Journal of Travels to Seringapatam, the Maldives, Puloo Penang, and Bengal, 1804-1805.
Letter to Sir G. H. Barlow, 1807.
Letter to W. B. Bayley, 1808. *Copy.*
Letter to Col. Richardson.
Letter to, from D. Erskine, 1809.
Letter to, from Lieut. F. Irvine, 1810.

Advocates' Library, Edinburgh.

Leyden (Dr John). Copy of the Tunes in Tablature in John Leyden's MS. Lyra-viol Book.
> Transcribed by George Farquhar Graham from the original MS., formerly in the possession of Andrew Leyden.

Thomas Morton, M.D., London.

Rhymed Letter addressed to Alex. Braidwood [August 3, 1795].
Letter to Alex. Braidwood, *circa* 1795.

BIBLIOGRAPHY

Letter to Thomas Logan, *circa* 1795.

Letters to Dr Thomas Brown from St Andrews in the winter and spring of 1797-8.

Letter to Dr Thomas Brown from Caldershall, September 1799.

Journal of a Tour to Gilsland and the Cumberland Lakes, June 1800.

Letter to Dr Thomas Brown from Oban, August 1800.

Letter to Miss Janet Brown, February 6, 1801.

Letter to James Morton (making suggestions as to his studies), July 6, 1802.

Verses to J[anet] B[rown] from J[ohn] L[eyden], *circa* 1802.

Letters to his brother Robert from London and Portsmouth, in one of which he mentions that the Marquis of Abercorn "carried him to Court," 1803.

Letter to Miss Janet Brown from Portsmouth, 1803.

Letter to his father from Madras, March 23, 1804.

Letter to William Erskine from Nunjengod, September 1804.

Letter to William Erskine from Seringapatam, November 1804.

Letter to Mr, afterwards Sir Stamford, Raffles from Calcutta, March 7, 1805.

Letter to William Erskine from Cananore, May 28, 1805.

Letter to William Erskine from Seringapatam, May 1805.

Letter to William Erskine from Calicut, July 4, 1805.

Letter to William Erskine from Quilon, September 9, 1805.

Letter to Richard Heber from Puloo Penang, October 1805.

Letter to his father from Puloo Penang, November 20, 1805.

Letter to Miss Janet Brown from Puloo Penang, 1805.
Letter to William Erskine from Penang, in which he describes the circumstances in which the ode to his Malay Krees was penned, December 1805.
Letter to William Erskine from Penang, January 1806.
Letter to Richard Heber from Calcutta, June 1806.
Letters to Mrs Raffles in 1806, 1808, and 1810.
Letter to William Erskine from Saugor Roads, June 1, 1807.
Leyden's Memorandum in reply to Sir W. Burrough's attack upon him, August 10, 1808.
Extracts from letter to William Erskine from Calcutta, May 15, 1809.
Extracts from letter to William Erskine from Chinsurah, July 29, 1809.
Extract from letter to William Erskine, dated Calcutta, December 30, 1809.
Letters to his father from Calcutta, January and August 1809 and January 1811.
Letter to William Erskine from Calcutta, July 15, 1810.
Letter to his father from the ship Phœnix, in the latitude of Masulipatam, on his way to Java, March 20, 1811.
Letter to Dr John Hare, Junr., from Madras, April 23, 1811.
Letter to Dr John Hare, Junr., from Malacca, June 13, 1811.
MS. copy of the ode on the Battle of Corunna.

> Endorsed by Mr Erskine: "The copy from which the above is taken is in Leyden's handwriting, and is addressed on the outside 'for Mrs Raffles.'"

Ode from the Persic of Rafiel'din.

Ode from the Persic of Jami.
> Marked in the MS. by Mr Erskine, "From, I suppose, Mrs Raffles' handwriting."

Prologue à la Militaire to 'Speed the Plough'; to be spoken in the character of a Serjeant going the rounds at an outpost at Barrackpore. (In verse.)
> Attested by Mr Erskine to be "from Leyden's handwriting."

Sonnet in 1800. J. L.
> Supposed to be in handwriting of Mrs Raffles. Mr Erskine appends the following interesting note:—
> "This, I think, is a translation from Petrarch or Werter. Leyden, one winter at Edinburgh, engaged in a friendly controversy with a young lady of refined poetical taste to decide which could write the best sonnet. The contest went on till each had written twelve. It was concluded by two of his friends writing a thirteenth in his name, overloaded with some of the peculiarities of his diction. This sounds to my ear as one of the number. Some of them were very beautiful, but he complained of the partiality of his judges, who decided against him.—W. E."

John Morton, M.D., Guildford, Surrey.

Letter to Mr Thomas Morton from Edinburgh, April 14, 1796.

Letter to Mr Thomas Brown and friends from St Andrews, describing habits and customs of the students, gown-stealing, &c., November 14, 1797.

Letter to Mr Thomas Brown from St Andrews, in which he mentions pleasure of meeting Dr Hunter and Mr Baron, December 1797.

Amusing and clever letter to Mr Thomas Brown from St Andrews, February 19, 1798.

Interesting letter to Mr Thomas Brown, St Patrick's Square, Edinburgh, from St Andrews, March 25, 1798.

Letter to Mr Thomas Brown and Mrs Brown from St Andrews. Commences, "My dear Friends, I have not advanced as far in clericality as to think that every heterodox son of a —— Church or State ought not only to be hanged, drawn, and quartered, but to be offered a whole burnt-offering to the God of mercy, as our good brethren and allies of Portugal do." April 17, 1798.

Letter to his father and mother from Edinburgh in answer to a complaint as to his writing so seldom, October 6, 1798.

Letter to his father from Edinburgh. Is sending medicine. Protest against his brother Robert being sent back to the farm for harvest. August 7, 1799.

Letter to Mr Thomas Brown from Calder Hall. Is to preach at Kirknewton on the Sunday next, the sermon to be extemporary. September 14, 1799.

Letter to Mr Thomas Brown and Mrs Brown from Oban, 7 A.M. Visit to Staffa, Inveraray, &c. July 25, 1800.

Letter to Mr Heber. Contents of MS. Volume of Ancient Romances in the Advocates' Library. Edinburgh [1800].

Letter to his father on private affairs, July 30 [1801].

Letter to his brother Robert. Mentions having a violent inflammation of the eyes. Rest of letter private matters. January 12 [1802].

Letter to his father about money matters in connection with his uncle Andrew, who died in America, July 30 [1802].

Letter to Richard Heber, Esq., concerning Irish literature, 1802.

Letter to his brother Robert from 43 Southampton Buildings, Holborn, London. Directs him to send some material to the printer Ballantyne; more to-morrow. Will sail to Cape of Good Hope about

by Lord Castlereagh, Lord Malmsbury, Lord Cavan, the Marquis of Abercorn, and the Portland family. Asks that his Highland Journal may be sent to him if it can possibly be procured. "I want it for various reasons, and, among others, for the account of Bruce's Abyssinian MSS." [February 1802.]

Letter to his father from the Isle of Wight. "Was presented at Court by Marquis of Abercorn, and was introduced to Lord Wm. Bentinck." April 15, 1803.

Letter to his father from Pulo Penang. Relates that when ill he lived in one of the palaces of Tippoo Sahib. November 20, 1806.

Letter to his father and mother from Calcutta. Says he has often in Court to speak seven languages in the same day. August 2, 1809.

Letter to the Rev. D. White, Arabic Professor, Oxford, from Calcutta. December 4, 1809.

Letter to Mr Haber from Calcutta accompanying a dissertation on the Chinese language. December 13, 1809.

Letter to Dr Leyden from Henry Carter, Barrackpore, August 26, 1810.

Letter to his father from Calcutta, January 2, 1811.

Letter to his father on his journey to Java from ship Phoenix, in the latitude of Masulipatam (imperfect), March 20, 1811.

Letter (mutilated) to his father per ship Sovereign, 1811.

lates that he was employed by Lord Minto, who,

he says, has been very kind to him. Had some fighting with hill robbers.

Fragments of the 'Story of Ganesa,' from the Mahratta.

Tales of the Peries. The History of Azar Shah, from the Persian.

Tragic Ballads. These appear to be variations picked up by Leyden, and differing materially from the published collections—

    The Cruel Brother, or the Bride's Testament.
    Lady Maisry.
    Burd Ellen.
    Bonny Bee Horn.

List of Manuscripts belonging to the estate of Dr John Leyden that were received by Wm. Erskine, Esq., from Mrs Cholmondeley, the executrix of the late Richard Heber, Esq.

Mr A. H. Millar, Dundee.

Drummond's Polemo-Middinia, Translation of the opening passage in. [By John Leyden.]

Mr James Sinton, Eastfield, Musselburgh.

Leyden, John. Journal of a Tour in the North of Scotland in 1800.

    The Rev. James Morton, in his Memoir of Leyden referring to this Journal, describes it as a Tour in the Highlands and Western Islands, and I have adopted that title as representing more correctly those parts of the Highlands he visited.—J. S.

—— On the Sabbath Morning. (Sonnet.)
—— Love. Written in 1800. (Sonnet.)

Abbotsford.

(For kindly furnishing me with the following list of MSS. at Abbotsford, I am indebted to Mr William Macmath.—J. S.)

MSS. in the handwriting of John Leyden, in volume titled 'Scotch Ballads: Materials for Border Minstrelsy':—

[No. 90.] Archie o' Ca'field. Variations. [85 lines.]
[No. 90*a*.] The Queen's Marie [Mary Hamilton]. [28 lines.]
[No. 96.] Thomas the Rhymer. Variations. [Got from] J. Ormiston, Kelso. [36 lines.]
[No. 96*a*.] Tamlane. [8 lines.]

No. 22*b*, in the same volume, is The Earl o' Bran [Earl Brand], in the handwriting of Richard Heber, who notes at the end: "I have not written the Chorus, but Mr Leyden, having it by him, knows how to insert it."

No. 127 is "Hold your hand, Lord Judge, she says" [The Maid freed from the Gallows], in a handwriting unknown, but addressed on the back to "Mr John Leydon, at Mr Scott's, Cabinet Maker, Lawson's Wynd, Laurieston, Edinburgh. Favour'd by Mr Smith."

The whole of the before-mentioned pieces are printed in 'The English and Scottish Popular Ballads,' edited by Francis James Child.

Mr Macmath has only a note of one letter at Abbotsford from Leyden to Scott, being doubtless the only one he could find relating to ballads. It is No. 84 of vol. i. of Letters addressed to Scott, and is headed "43 Southampton Buildings, Holborn." It is undated, but placed February 1803.

" . . . I have got from Ritson the Rookhope Ryde, which I think you saw, which he has added to his Durham Ballads, which I will send you if you think proper. It may go into a note in the third vol., but you had best write him about its insertion, for I imagine he is not well pleased that you anticipated him in the Solport fray [The Fray of Suport], and he says Prince Robert is clearly a Bishopric Ballad, the names of places being the same. . . ."